HALO 4
THE ESSENTIAL VISUAL GUIDE

CONTENTS

CHARACTERS

CAMPAIGN

SPARTAN OPS

FACTIONS

HUMAN

COVENANT

PROMETHEAN

WEAPONS

HUMAN

COVENANT

FORERUNNER

VEHICLES

HUMAN

NON-HUMAN

INTRODUCTION

Halo 4 was the product of many incredibly talented people across a wide spectrum of trades and skill sets coming together for one singular purpose: the return of the legendary Master Chief. After five long years, the central figure of the Halo Universe has awakened to face an ancient threat more powerful than anything that has come before. And although this Spartan is a founding part of the Halo story, anyone who has played through Halo 4 will quickly recognize that this universe's walls extend far beyond just one man, or even one species.

Halo 4: The Essential Visual Guide's humble goal is to catalogue as much of the epic, galaxy-spanning Halo 4 experience—including its addictive War Games and its intense Spartan Ops episodes—as physically possible within the covers of this book. We will explore characters, weapons, vehicles, armor, ships, and much more; objects both new and old, both immense and intricate, will be elaborated upon within the pages that follow. So pull up a chair and prepare to dive into the deepest and most expansive guide ever created for Halo 4.

CHARACTERS

MASTER CHIEF

MASTER CHIEF PETTY OFFICER JOHN-117

Conscripted into the SPARTAN-II program as a child, the boy named John would be physically augmented and encased in Mjolnir battle armor, ultimately becoming the Master Chief. For three decades, this Spartan would battle against the Covenant, eventually making the critical discovery of Halo and tipping the scales in humanity's favor. But in the aftermath of the war, the Chief would find the human race threatened by another force—an ancient Forerunner known as the Didact. Although the Spartan would prevail, this conflict would not come without a loss: Cortana, the Chief's artificial construct and ally, would perish in battle.

Integrated heads-up display

Protective underarmor mesh

Magnetic hardpoint to mount sidearm

Modified Mjolnir Mark VI armor

STATISTICS

NAME	**HEIGHT**
John-117	7ft 2in (218cm)
AFFILIATION	**WEIGHT**
UNSC	286.6lbs (130kg)
RANK	**BIRTHWORLD**
Master Chief Petty Officer	Eridanus II
SERVICE NUMBER	**DATE OF BIRTH**
S-117	March 7, 2511

Fully updated by Cortana, this armor resembles an earlier line of Mjolnir Mark IV.

CORTANA

CTN 0452-9

Created from the mind of Dr. Catherine Halsey, Cortana is a unique AI construct, as she was designed using the neural pathways of a living human. In 2552, she was paired with the Master Chief for Operation: RED FLAG, but the sudden fall of the planet Reach would set the two on a collision course with Halo. The discovery of this ancient ringworld would not only bring victory in the war against the Covenant, but it would also lead to the reemergence of the Didact—an ancient Forerunner with a vicious hatred of humanity. During a battle aboard the Didact's ship, Cortana would ultimately perish, sacrificing her life to stop this new enemy.

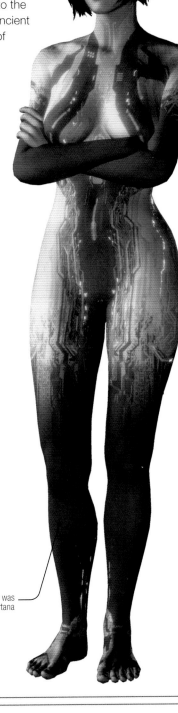

Neural architecture from Halsey

Physical shape was chosen by Cortana

Cortana suffered from rampancy, a volatile state of instability smart AIs encounter after seven years of service.

STATISTICS

NAME Cortana	**HEIGHT** N/A
AFFILIATION UNSC	**WEIGHT** N/A
RANK Artificial Intelligence	**ACTIVATION SITE** Reach
SERVICE NUMBER CTN 0452-9	**ACTIVATION DATE** November 7, 2549

CAPTAIN DEL RIO

CAPTAIN ANDREW DEL RIO

With an impressive naval career and a strong focus on results, Andrew Del Rio appeared to be an easy choice for captain of the UNSC *Infinity* on its inaugural voyage. Yet, despite this, his actions during the conflict on Requiem would prove costly for the UNSC. Del Rio would abandon the Master Chief and Cortana to face the Didact alone, cutting his losses and salvaging what remained of *Infinity*'s forces. Upon returning to Earth, UNSC High Command would remove Del Rio from this post and replace him with Thomas Lasky, *Infinity*'s XO (Executive Officer), who would aid the Chief when the Didact inevitably assaulted Earth.

UNSC Navy rank of Captain

Unified Earth Government emblem

Soft case for personal effects

Standard Navy dress slacks

Del Rio's abandonment of the Master Chief and Cortana would ultimately cost him his role on *Infinity*.

STATISTICS

NAME
Andrew Del Rio

HEIGHT
5ft 11in (180cm)

AFFILIATION
UNSC

WEIGHT
210lbs (95.3kg)

RANK
Captain

BIRTHWORLD
Earth

SERVICE NUMBER
90302-75627-AD

DATE OF BIRTH
May 28, 2500

CAPTAIN LASKY

CAPTAIN THOMAS LASKY

Due to his mother's high status in the UNSC, Thomas Lasky was destined for military service, even if he viewed the colonial insurrection as ethically problematic when he began training at the Corbulo Academy of Military Science (CAMS). It would be the Covenant's assault on the colony of Circinius IV that would launch him into an accomplished military career and eventually the position of XO of the UNSC *Infinity*. During the events on Requiem, he would assist in the Master Chief's and Cortana's fight against the Didact, eventually rising to serve as *Infinity*'s commanding officer when the Forerunner assaulted the Earth, and later when *Infinity* returned to the world of Requiem.

STATISTICS

NAME	**HEIGHT**
Thomas Lasky	5ft 11in (182cm)
AFFILIATION	**WEIGHT**
UNSC	169lbs (76.7kg)
RANK	**BIRTHWORLD**
Captain	Mars
SERVICE NUMBER	**DATE OF BIRTH**
98604-72690-TL	August 15, 2510

Extensive training at CAMS prepared Lasky for the challenges he would inevitably encounter later.

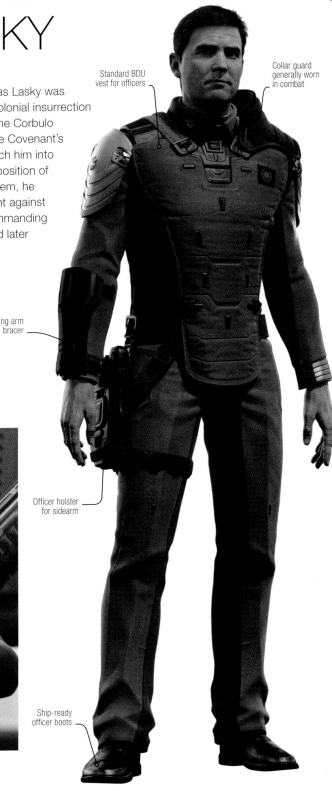

Standard BDU vest for officers

Collar guard generally worn in combat

Firing arm bracer

Officer holster for sidearm

Ship-ready officer boots

Halsey's interactions with the Covenant would ultimately make her a target of the UNSC.

Bullet wound forced arm amputation by Jul 'Mdama

Thick, flame-resistant lab gear

DOCTOR HALSEY

DOCTOR CATHERINE HALSEY

Contracted by ONI (Office of Naval Intelligence) at a young age, the prodigy known as Catherine Halsey would spearhead the SPARTAN-II and MJOLNIR projects, as well as the creation of the remarkable AI, Cortana. Moral ambiguities regarding these programs would, however, call into question the doctor's ethics, eventually leading to her arrest on the Forerunner world of Onyx. Nevertheless, ONI would still utilize Halsey to help integrate the UNSC *Infinity*'s Forerunner engines, as well as analyze a number of Forerunner artifacts. During *Infinity*'s campaign on Requiem, Halsey would be abducted by the Covenant, though her allegiances are deeply questioned by the UNSC.

STATISTICS

NAME	**HEIGHT**
Catherine Halsey	5ft 7in (170.2cm)
AFFILIATION	**WEIGHT**
N/A	117lbs (53kg)
RANK	**BIRTHWORLD**
N/A	Endymion
SERVICE NUMBER	**DATE OF BIRTH**
CC-409871	March 19, 2492

Lab-grade footwear

DOCTOR TILLSON

DOCTOR SANDRA TILLSON

Born on the Outer Colony of Coral, Sandra Tillson earned a scholarship to the esteemed Pegasi Institute. One of only a handful of experts in the field of Xenoarchaeology, she was hired by the Office of Naval Intelligence to conduct research on a number of sites later determined to be of Forerunner origin. When Installation 03 was discovered, Tillson was the first to be integrated into the research team on Ivanoff Station, and she would be the one responsible for the discovery of the Composer. This find would ultimately end in tragedy, as the Didact would use it against Tillson and all who served on Ivanoff.

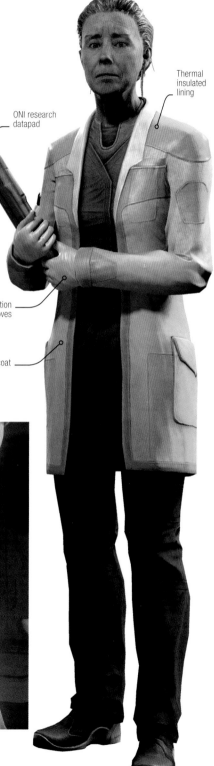

Thermal insulated lining

ONI research datapad

Sterile manipulation gloves

Standard ONI lab coat

STATISTICS

NAME	**HEIGHT**
Sandra Tillson	5ft 9in (175.3cm)
AFFILIATION	**WEIGHT**
UNSC	131lbs (59.4kg)
RANK	**BIRTHWORLD**
N/A	Coral
SERVICE NUMBER	**DATE OF BIRTH**
CC-728304	May 14, 2506

Tillson was eventually forced to relinquish years of research in an attempt to halt the Didact's destructive plans.

STATISTICS

NAME
Shadow-of-Sundered-Star

AFFILIATION
Forerunner

RANK
N/A

SERVICE NUMBER
N/A

HEIGHT
11ft 4in (345.4cm)

WEIGHT
794.9lbs (360.6kg)

BIRTHWORLD
N/A

DATE OF BIRTH
N/A

Six-fingered hand
of Warrior-Servant

Warrior body-
assist armor

Despite the
Librarian's hope
otherwise, the
Didact's time in
the Cryptum
only fed his
malice for
humanity.

Armor
spontaneously
adheres to body

THE DIDACT

PROTECTOR OF ECUMENE

An ancient Forerunner commander, the Didact was once
the victim of a political conflict with another sect of
Forerunners. Forced into a Cryptum, he would later be
awakened only to be abandoned in a Flood-infested
system where he encountered the Gravemind. This event
would ultimately turn him from warrior champion to
heartless monster—leading him to using the Composer
against innocent humans, transforming them into machine
warriors called Prometheans. Though he would unwillingly
be forced back into another Cryptum, his return one
hundred thousand years later would revive his long-
dormant hatred of humans. His fate after the cataclysmic
battle with the Master Chief remains a mystery.

The Librarian provided Halsey with the Janus Key shortly before Requiem was sent into its sun.

Head-covering of repose

Ancilla receptacle

The Librarian's presence on Requiem was a cognitive imprint, capable only of limited interactivity.

Node manipulator

THE LIBRARIAN

LIFESHAPER OF ECUMENE

The Lifeworker known as the Librarian was a Forerunner without equal during their war with the Flood. Wife to the warrior Didact and prolific Lifeshaper (leader of all Lifeworkers), the Librarian would spearhead the Conservation Measure, a massive effort to save all sentient life in the galaxy from the devastating Flood parasite and the destruction caused by the Halo Array. Although she would save many species, she could not save herself—she became a victim of Halo while on Earth. However, her belief that humans should inherit the Mantle fueled her actions at the very end of the war, eventually helping the Master Chief gain victory over her twisted husband.

Conveyance dais

STATISTICS

NAME First-Light-Weaves-Living-Song	**HEIGHT** 9ft 6in (289.6cm)
AFFILIATION Forerunner	**WEIGHT** 441.4lbs (200.2kg)
RANK N/A	**BIRTHWORLD** N/A
SERVICE NUMBER N/A	**DATE OF BIRTH** N/A

Mjolnir SCOUT armor

M6H PDWS

COMMANDER PALMER

COMMANDER SARAH PALMER

Sarah Palmer was one of the first recruits within ONI's top secret SPARTAN-IV project, despite having already served twelve tours of duty across eight different worlds as a marine. Palmer was an obvious choice for the program for a variety of reasons, most important of which was her impressive leadership ability. When the UNSC *Infinity* set out, Sarah would serve as Spartan Commander—leader of all Spartan-IVs aboard the massive vessel. Not only would Palmer participate in the early encounters on Requiem, but she would also command the Spartan forces as they returned several months later, eventually recovering an ancient Forerunner artifact called the Janus Key.

Standard S-IV configuration

Despite her administrative role as Spartan Commander, Palmer is no stranger to combat.

Roland was a critical fixture of UNSC *Infinity*'s presence and activity on Requiem.

WWII fighter pilot garb

STATISTICS

NAME	**HEIGHT**
Roland	N/A
AFFILIATION	**WEIGHT**
UNSC	N/A
RANK	**ACTIVATION SITE**
Artificial Intelligence	Earth
SERVICE NUMBER	**ACTIVATION DATE**
RLD 0205-4	December 5, 2557

ROLAND

RLD 0205-4

Roland is an extremely capable and proficient smart AI construct. He replaced the UNSC *Infinity*'s previous AI, who was destroyed when the ship crashed on the surface of Requiem in 2557. Choosing to visualize himself as a veteran World War II pilot, Roland's bravado and candor may have originated from his neural donor, or is perhaps his favored personality profile. Nevertheless, despite this cocksure attitude, he has remained incredibly reliable during events of meteoric significance, including the protracted campaign that took place on the shield world of Requiem and the recovery of a number of Forerunner artifacts of great importance.

Projected light composition

Mjolnir RECRUIT armor

THORNE

SPARTAN GABRIEL THORNE

Born on Earth, Gabriel Thorne enlisted in the UNSC Army at a young age. After the battle of Criterion, where he singlehandedly saved his entire platoon, Thorne fought on both Tribute and Reach, before ending up on Mars, where he served under the renowned Colonel Ackerson. Thorne's steely courage and tactical awareness allowed him access into the SPARTAN-IV program—though his entry was spurred by the Didact's assault on New Phoenix, his family having been victims of the attack. Joining Fireteam Majestic in early 2558, Thorne would be deployed to Requiem in the UNSC's effort to research it.

STATISTICS

NAME
Gabriel Thorne

HEIGHT
6ft 10in (208.1cm)

AFFILIATION
UNSC

WEIGHT
272lbs (123.4kg)

RANK
Spartan

BIRTHWORLD
Earth

SERVICE NUMBER
83920-91083-GT

DATE OF BIRTH
July 5, 2534

MA5D ICWS

Power conduit on cuisse system

Segmented plates increase mobility

As he is relatively new to SPARTAN-IV, Thorne still dons RECRUIT armor.

Tech suit base

Mjolnir SOLDIER armor

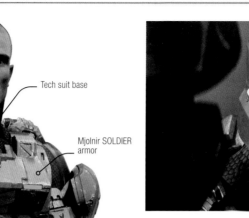

DeMarco's choice of SOLDIER armor is a result of extensive field experience.

Fixed soft cases

STATISTICS	
NAME Paul DeMarco	**HEIGHT** 7ft 1in (216.3cm)
AFFILIATION UNSC	**WEIGHT** 280lbs (127.1kg)
RANK Spartan	**BIRTHWORLD** Algolis
SERVICE NUMBER 76283-34092-PD	**DATE OF BIRTH** August 24, 2532

DEMARCO

SPARTAN PAUL DEMARCO

Brash and abrasive, the leader of Fireteam Majestic is none other than Paul DeMarco, a battle-hardened ODST who was born and raised on the colony of Algolis. After several years of service, DeMarco was recruited to become a Spartan. Analysts concluded that his tactical skill and talent were invaluable, even in light of his coarse and sometimes irreverent behavior. Deployed in a number of locations before his current assignment, DeMarco's immediate role on Majestic is fireteam leader, and despite the arduous challenges they've faced during *Infinity*'s protracted campaign on Requiem, he has carried his team well.

Shield emitter junction

Heavy-plated boot

HOYA

SPARTAN CARLO HOYA

Refugees from the planet Asmara, Carlo Hoya and his family knew firsthand the devastation possible at the hands of the Covenant. After finding sanctuary on the Inner Colony of Circumstance and reaching the eligible age, Carlo didn't hesitate to join the Marines. There he quickly advanced, eventually becoming an ODST and engaging the Covenant across several theaters. During the Battle of New Jerusalem, Hoya was taken prisoner by the Covenant, but managed to escape, saving a dozen naval officers in the process. Despite his short fuse and his tendency toward recklessness, his brazen actions eventually won him a placement as a Spartan-IV.

Mjolnir OPERATOR armor

Low-set reactor pack

M45D TS

RECRUIT greave system

Hoya's close-quarters combat skills are often eclipsed by his temerity in the field.

STATISTICS

NAME Carlo Hoya	**HEIGHT** 7ft 1in (216.1cm)
AFFILIATION UNSC	**WEIGHT** 281lbs (127.4kg)
RANK Spartan	**BIRTHWORLD** Asmara
SERVICE NUMBER 90302-89202-CH	**DATE OF BIRTH** December 15, 2533

MADSEN

SPARTAN ANTHONY MADSEN

Despite being the eldest Spartan on Fireteam Majestic, Anthony Madsen had previously led a somewhat undistinguished career in Marine Corps. His recruitment into SPARTAN-IV wasn't the result of any particular accomplishment, but rather nepotism, as both his father and grandfather were generals in the Corps. As a Spartan, Madsen passionately believes his performance here will ultimately dictate his legacy, hopefully salvaging a rather lackluster military career. Though Spartan-IVs bear no formal rank, Madsen is considered second-in-command to DeMarco on Majestic, simply for his duration of service on the fireteam.

Mjolnir RECON armor

SRS99-S5

Exposed shield conduits

Off-market RECON greave system

STATISTICS	
NAME	Anthony Madsen
AFFILIATION	UNSC
RANK	Spartan
SERVICE NUMBER	75283-56282-AM
HEIGHT	6ft 10in (209cm)
WEIGHT	278lbs (126.1kg)
BIRTHWORLD	New Llanelli
DATE OF BIRTH	October 19, 2530

Madsen's primary combat specialization is forward deployment and scouting.

STATISTICS

NAME
Tedra Grant

AFFILIATION
UNSC

RANK
Spartan

SERVICE NUMBER
95984-78393-TG

HEIGHT
6ft 9in (206cm)

WEIGHT
239lbs (108.4kg)

BIRTHWORLD
Arcadia

DATE OF BIRTH
November 4, 2533

GRANT

SPARTAN TEDRA GRANT

Arcadian by birth, Tedra Grant joined the UNSC Navy at a young age, having grown up in a harsh world that had already been attacked by the Covenant in 2531. Her impressive athletic ability and her innate combat skills would eventually gain her access into an operational division, field-testing early versions of the Mjolnir GEN2 armor. Shortly after this, she would accept a position as an active Spartan before joining Fireteam Majestic. Despite being a remarkable soldier, Grant's best talents are her sharp insight and clear decision-making. She remains calm and devoted to the task at hand, no matter how harried the situation may be.

Mjolnir PATHFINDER armor

Extended canopy mount

IMBR-119
Close-fitting
pauldron to
optimize mobility

Specialized channel-
locked vambrace

M395 DMR

Baseline RECRUIT
greave system

Grant's unique combat skills helped assist Majestic in securing key Forerunner artifacts.

DOCTOR GLASSMAN

DOCTOR HENRY GLASSMAN

Henry Glassman gained ONI's attention early in his career with his work in astrophysics and quantum theory. Several of Glassman's proposals aided the UNSC's refinement of translight travel and he was quickly integrated into ONI's B5D experimental research group, and eventually offered a position on the UNSC *Infinity* when its crew was secretly assembled. Despite friction between their personalities, Glassman would work with Dr. Catherine Halsey to install the vessel's Forerunner-based slipspace engines, forever altering translight travel for humanity. During *Infinity*'s protracted campaign on Requiem, Glassman was briefly captured by the Covenant, a scenario that would eventually lead the UNSC to the discovery of the mysterious Janus Key artifact.

Treated harshly by the Covenant

Covenant explosives vest

Verdant, patchwork lab slacks

Glassman's curiosity would lead the UNSC to recover part of the Janus Key.

STATISTICS

NAME
Henry Glassman

AFFILIATION
UNSC

RANK
N/A

SERVICE NUMBER
CC-652562

HEIGHT
6ft (183.4cm)

WEIGHT
180lbs (81.6kg)

BIRTHWORLD
New Carthage

DATE OF BIRTH
February 1, 2522

ONI's officer BDU

Data/comm
device

Protective
officer slacks

**After years of
reluctance, Osman
finally gives the order
to terminate Halsey.**

ADMIRAL OSMAN

ADMIRAL SERIN OSMAN

Serin Osman's past is something of a mystery. Previously, she was publicly known as the protégé of CINCONI Margaret Parangosky, though now she has taken over this role as an admiral, with full authority of the Office of Naval Intelligence. Secretly, however, Osman's past was in the SPARTAN-II program. She was a victim of failed physical augmentations, eventually saved by Parangosky and integrated back into the UNSC Navy. She would go on to head Kilo-Five, a highly classified black ops team used to destabilize remnants of the Covenant, thereby preventing another war. As CINCONI, Osman would eventually give the green light to terminate Catherine Halsey, the doctor's recent activity having made her an enemy of the state.

STATISTICS

NAME Serin Osman	**HEIGHT** 6ft 3in (190.8cm)
AFFILIATION UNSC	**WEIGHT** 189lbs (86.7kg)
RANK Admiral	**BIRTHWORLD** N/A
SERVICE NUMBER 39489-72738-SO	**DATE OF BIRTH** N/A

'Mdama acquired
one half of the Janus
Key, while the UNSC
has the other.

Holographic
symbol denotes
leadership

JUL 'MDAMA

THE HAND OF THE DIDACT

At the end of the Covenant War, Jul 'Mdama was belligerent to the pro-human movement spearheaded by the Arbiter, which inevitably led to an affiliation with the extremist sect called Servants of the Abiding Truth. During the events that followed, 'Mdama would be abducted by humans and locked away on the shield world of Onyx, only to escape through a Forerunner portal to Hesduros—a Sangheili frontier world where he would initiate his campaign to awaken the ancient Forerunner known as the Didact. Now called the "Hand of the Didact," this Sangheili leads an extremely fanatic resurrection of the former Covenant, fiercely attempting to uncover all of Requiem's deepest secrets.

Zealot-class cuisse

Prong-claw is
entirely ornamental

STATISTICS

NAME
Jul 'Mdama

AFFILIATION
Covenant

RANK
Supreme Commander

SERVICE NUMBER
N/A

HEIGHT
7ft 10in (239.9cm)

WEIGHT
324lbs (146.9kg)

BIRTHWORLD
Sanghelios

DATE OF BIRTH
March 5, 2489

Standard Sangheili
combat harness

GEK 'LHAR

COMMANDER GEK 'LHAR

Born on the island of Alytcos, just off the northern shores of Kaepra, the Sangheili field commander known as Gek 'Lhar served for decades during the Covenant's campaign against humans, only to watch the military powerhouse crushed under the weight of the Great Schism. 'Lhar was a ruthless warrior within the Covenant, but his service to Jul 'Mdama (and by proxy, the Didact's cause) is unwavering and incredibly fervent, only matched by his hatred for humans. In fact, 'Lhar has collected the dog tags of the Spartans he has killed, often adorning them on his person as evidence of his ferocity. During the final days of the UNSC's campaign on Requiem, 'Lhar would be killed by Fireteam Majestic.

Energy
sword

STATISTICS	
NAME Gek 'Lhar	**HEIGHT** 8ft (245.3cm)
AFFILIATION Covenant	**WEIGHT** 327lbs (148.3kg)
RANK Commander	**BIRTHWORLD** Sanghelios
SERVICE NUMBER N/A	**DATE OF BIRTH** October 19, 2499

Form-fitted
Sangheili greave

Losing the human prisoner Glassman would ultimately cost 'Lhar his life.

PARG VOL

COMMANDER PARG VOL

Sangheili terrorist born and bred on the base world of Malurok (also called Decided Heart), Parg Vol was once a field master within the Covenant guard until its demise shortly after the Great Schism. Although he despised the Jiralhanae and San'Shyuum, he also opposed the Arbiter's alliance with humanity and believed that the Sangheili should have wiped them out completely. After the war, Vol would dabble in arms deals and hit contracts before consolidating a small task force under the leadership of Jul 'Mdama. Vol has never been passionately religious, but his volatile hatred for humans has aligned with 'Mdama's cause extremely well. Parg Vol would be eventually targeted and killed by Fireteam Crimson.

Elaborate Warrior-class helmet

Vol often carries a heavy weapon for personal protection.

Raised-claw armor is largely ornamental

High-framed Sangheili greave

STATISTICS

NAME
Parg Vol

AFFILIATION
Covenant

RANK
Commander

SERVICE NUMBER
N/A

HEIGHT
8ft 3in (251.6cm)

WEIGHT
342lbs (155.1kg)

BIRTHWORLD
Malurok

DATE OF BIRTH
July 24, 2481

FACTIONS

MARINES

UNITED NATIONS SPACE COMMAND

The United Nations Space Command and the Marine Corps, its primary combat force, were created in the 22nd century during the brief but violent Interplanetary Wars. Although it was retained within the Sol system during the interstellar colonial surges of the 23rd century, it would gain prominence across all human colonies after the reduction of the CMA (Colonial Military Administration) amid political scandal. Despite being only one of a number of branches within the UNSC, the Marines are not only the largest and most versatile combat force deployed, but they are also considered the most significant groundside factor during the course of the war (aside from the Spartans).

Post-Covenant War troopers utilize a larger BDU variety than previous generations.

Off-world Marine helmet

Standard Marine BDU

Resilient boot-greave

STANDARD INFANTRY

STATISTICS

AFFILIATION
UNSC

HOMEWORLD
Earth

HEIGHT RANGE
5ft 9in–6ft 2in (175–188cm)

WEIGHT RANGE
141–204lbs (64–92.5kg)

HEAVY INFANTRY

MEDIC

FIELD SERGEANT

By 2557, there were already several hundred Spartan-IVs in active service.

Baseline RECRUIT helmet

Fusion reactor pack

Firing-arm pauldron

S-IV assets used Mjolnir [GEN2] armor

Standard RECRUIT greave

SPARTANS

UNITED NATIONS SPACE COMMAND

The Spartan branch is largely comprised of SPARTAN-IV personnel, though its roots flow deep into the SPARTAN-II and SPARTAN-III programs that preceded it. Without question, they are the most elite infantry force used by the UNSC, generally operating in a strict fireteam framework while leveraging augmented physical bodies and powered armor systems. Unlike other branches, which maintain escalating rank systems, all Spartans are considered equal, their standing and specialization determined by personal skill alone, whether in live combat or during War Games exercises. All detachments operate under a Spartan commander, while individual fireteams operate under a team leader; all of these are effectively balanced to optimize field performance.

STATISTICS

AFFILIATION
UNSC

HOMEWORLD
Earth

HEIGHT RANGE
6ft 9in–7ft 1in (206–216cm)

WEIGHT RANGE
239–281lbs (108.4–127.4kg)

ONI SECURITY

UNITED NATIONS SPACE COMMAND

The Office of Naval Intelligence maintains its own security force, generally comprised of recruited Army and Marine candidates. Their alignment under the UNSC Navy branch and jurisdictional placement within the Naval Special Warfare group afford them some autonomy, though ONI manages their operation. The security force maintained by Ivanoff Station was used primarily for science team protection on Gamma Halo and in the rare case of an emergency or attack. Unfortunately, such an attack would come, and with a force previously unimagined by ONI. In the process, all security personnel would be killed by Covenant invaders or composed when an ancient and powerful artifact was suddenly activated.

STATISTICS

AFFILIATION
UNSC

HOMEWORLD
Earth

HEIGHT RANGE
5ft 9in–6ft 2in (175–188cm)

WEIGHT RANGE
141–204lbs (64–92.5kg)

Reinforced pauldron for heavy combat

Off-world rebreather system

Specialized composite engineered by ONI

MA5D ICWS

ONI Security specializes in site protection and defense.

SCIENTISTS

UNITED NATIONS SPACE COMMAND

Most scientists within the Office of Naval Intelligence are privately contracted, as they are not part of administrative or combat elements. Despite this, ONI demands that all science personnel pass standardized weapon tests, in the unlikely event that combat will be needed. On the highly classified Ivanoff Station, ONI scientists were studying Gamma Halo and a number of important artifacts acquired from its surface. Tragically, a powerful Covenant assault force would lay siege to the station, resulting in the deaths of many despite their training. Nevertheless, a handful of scientists managed to narrowly escape into the system's asteroid field and were later saved by search and rescue teams.

Ivanoff played host to over a dozen different science disciplines.

STATISTICS

AFFILIATION
UNSC

HOMEWORLD
Earth

HEIGHT RANGE
5ft 9in–6ft 2in (175–188cm)

WEIGHT RANGE
141–204lbs (64–92.5kg)

Ship-grade lab wear

QUANTUM PHYSICIST

XENOARCHAEOLOGIST

Lab clogs

STORM GRUNT

COVENANT UNGGOY

The Storm Grunt class is the most common among Unggoy within the reestablished Covenant sect led by Jul 'Mdama. This class uses a standard battle harness with low-weight material for ease of mobility and functional awareness. In order to increase field of view, this role also employs a nose-placed rebreather that resembles diving apparatuses used on the Unggoy homeworld of Balaho. When encountered in low numbers, Storm Grunts are generally easy to dispatch—unfortunately, this class is almost always deployed in larger numbers or as augmentation to Sangheili and Kig-Yar detachments.

Storm Grunts represent little threat when encountered in low numbers.

STATISTICS

AFFILIATION
Covenant

HOMEWORLD
Balaho

HEIGHT RANGE
4ft 6.5in–5ft 7in (138.4–167cm)

WEIGHT RANGE
248.3–260.1lbs (112.6–118kg)

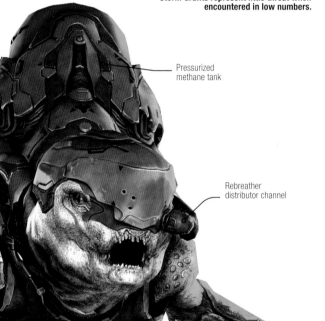

Pressurized
methane tank

Filter actuator

Rebreather
distributor channel

T-25 DEP

Hardened
membrane

IMPERIAL GRUNT

COVENANT UNGGOY

Designated by their service within the previous Covenant body, Imperial Grunts are experienced and battle-hardened troops who have been offered slightly higher placement in the current Unggoy hierarchy. Despite the fact that these soldiers are typically outfitted with standard infantry weapons, they often wear more resilient armor and protective face-shielding, providing them greater overall durability on the battlefield. Now, as the recently emerging Covenant faction gains permanence, it is unknown whether Imperial Grunts will maintain their current status or if they will be assimilated into the larger Unggoy population.

STATISTICS

AFFILIATION
Covenant

HOMEWORLD
Balaho

HEIGHT RANGE
4ft 6.5in–5ft 7in (138.4–167cm)

WEIGHT RANGE
248.3–260.1lbs (112.6–118kg)

Imperial Grunt scouts often augment standard patrols.

Tank resembles Balahoan octopoda

Heavy armor face plate

Scale-like membrane protects forearms

T-33 GML

Hardened claws

GRUNT RANGER

COVENANT UNGGOY

Referred to as Grunt Rangers by humans, these specialists are fully trained and heavily armored for extra-vehicular activity. They are typically deployed with high-strain engagement suits designed to withstand extreme temperatures, low-to-zero gravity, and other rigors found in the vacuum of space. The Grunt Ranger role, like all other Ranger elements within the Covenant, can also be deployed into terrestrial and standard gravity contexts, particularly where vertical mobility may be challenging for other classes due to difficulties in terrain, or in order to gain a tactical advantage against a grounded opposition.

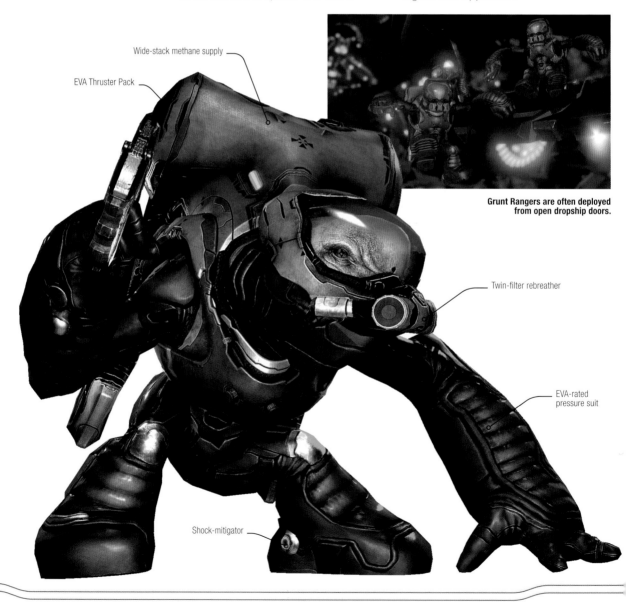

Grunt Rangers are often deployed from open dropship doors.

Wide-stack methane supply

EVA Thruster Pack

Twin-filter rebreather

EVA-rated pressure suit

Shock-mitigator

GRUNT HEAVY

COVENANT UNGGOY

The most impressive of all Unggoy delineations is the Grunt Heavy class, used to engage high-tier enemies through the use of augmented armor, explosives, and other volatile weapons. Grunt Heavy personnel wear full-face protective rebreathers, enhanced optical sensors, and robust battle harnesses in an effort to compensate for their lack of size and speed. As expected, this class is comprised of experienced and formidable Unggoy warriors, often fully capable of engaging even lightly armed vehicles effectively. Grunt Heavy units are rarely encountered on the battlefield, but opponents should observe extreme caution when they are spotted.

Grunt Heavy units are often experienced enough to accompany well-armored Elite fireteams.

STATISTICS

AFFILIATION
Covenant

HOMEWORLD
Balaho

HEIGHT RANGE
4ft 6.5in–5ft 7in (138.4–167cm)

WEIGHT RANGE
248.3–260.1lbs (112.6–118kg)

Analog eye sockets of Unggoy predator

Slim-stock tank

Scale-mottled, xeno-arthropod skin

Optics articulator

Squat, natural posture

Fully capable of weapon manipulation

Sharp claws for climbing and digging

STORM JACKAL

COVENANT KIG-YAR

Rising from the ashes of the previous Covenant, the newly formed alliance under Jul 'Mdama has instituted a number of changes across their lines—this includes the introduction of the Storm class, the front line of all Covenant infantry types. Storm Jackals are dominant in number among the Kig-Yar and are equipped with personal energy shields which provide solid yet versatile cover whenever needed. Storm Jackals generally operate in detachments of two or three, or alongside a Sangheili-led squad comprised of various species, although the Kig-Yar's individual autonomy allows them to be deployed alone if needed.

STATISTICS

AFFILIATION
Covenant

HOMEWORLD
Eayn

HEIGHT RANGE
6ft 2in–6ft 8in (190–203cm)

WEIGHT RANGE
195–206lbs (88–93kg)

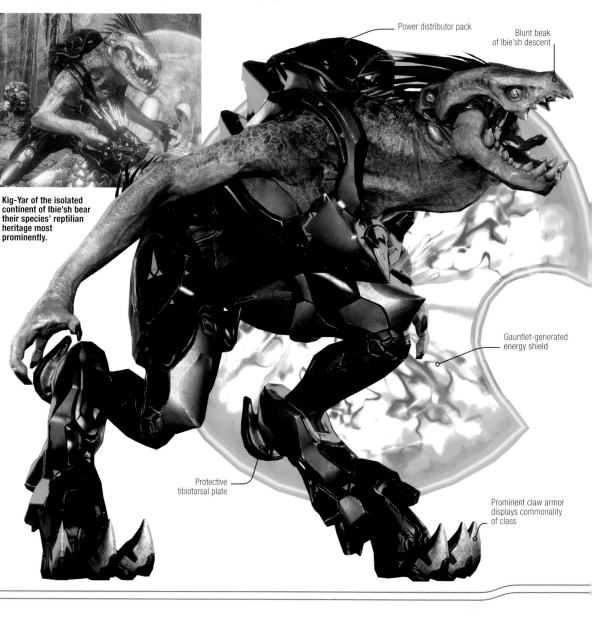

Kig-Yar of the isolated continent of Ibie'sh bear their species' reptilian heritage most prominently.

Power distributor pack

Blunt beak of Ibie'sh descent

Gauntlet-generated energy shield

Protective tibiotarsal plate

Prominent claw armor displays commonality of class

JACKAL RANGER

COVENANT KIG-YAR

A major component of the Covenant's extra-vehicular activity combat element, Jackal Rangers are agile and sleek—they are trained to execute missions in zero- and low-gravity circumstances. These Kig-Yar are sealed within heavily armored, EVA-enabled suits. Their arsenal primarily incorporates accurate marksman weapons such as the Covenant Carbine, advantaged by their impressive visual acuity. As with all Ranger classes, Jackal Rangers are designed for EVA context; however they can also operate in normal-gravity conditions where verticality (such as rocky inclines, trees, or even urban environments) is a component of combat.

STATISTICS

AFFILIATION
Covenant

HOMEWORLD
Eayn

HEIGHT RANGE
6ft 2in–6ft 8in (190–203cm)

WEIGHT RANGE
195–206lbs (88–93kg)

It's not uncommon to encounter Jackal Rangers operating as snipers.

EVA helmet

Low-collar chest armor typical of all Jackal classes

T-51 Carbine

Agile, bird-like posture

The Ranger's atmosphere-sealed EVA suit is particularly resilient.

Jackal Snipers aren't restricted to perches and often engage in direct combat on the ground.

Smart-linked sighting optics for extreme-range sniping

Pre-Avian male plumage

T-27 SASR

Channel muzzle

STATISTICS

AFFILIATION
Covenant

HOMEWORLD
Eayn

HEIGHT RANGE
6ft 2in–6ft 8in (190–203cm)

WEIGHT RANGE
195–206lbs (88–93kg)

JACKAL SNIPER

COVENANT KIG-YAR

Kig-Yar are born with innate abilities that have naturally suited them to the roles of scout and sniper in the Covenant military. Their lithe composition, their sturdy yet swift frame, and their deft mobility have all logically led to the formation of the Jackal Sniper class. Despite their physical advantages, this class is still outfitted with rugged armor and an ocular enhancement helmet, which is smart-linked to their weapon. This type of heavily improved visual optimization allows them to sight and target enemies at extreme distances, generally using a Covenant sniper rifle or other long-range marksman weapon.

JACKAL HEAVY

COVENANT KIG-YAR

Among the Kig-Yar contingent, Jackal Heavy is easily the strongest and most capable class for infantry warfare. Balancing both tactile dexterity with impressive armor and resilient portable energy shields, these Kig-Yar can pose an extremely challenging threat to any opposition. Jackal Heavy personnel are usually armed with munitions launchers and are integrated into any detachments that require heavy firepower, particularly those opposing lightly armed vehicles. The most remarkable aspect of the Kig-Yar Heavy class is its incorporation of the Needler, a weapon that, when used effectively, provides both precision and violently explosive results.

STATISTICS

AFFILIATION
Covenant

HOMEWORLD
Eayn

HEIGHT RANGE
6ft 2in–12ft 3in (190–203cm)

WEIGHT RANGE
195–206lbs (88–93kg)

Heavy-grade
helmet/collar

Feral maw
reveals Ibie'sh
ancestry

T-25 DEP

Shield cleft allows
firing optimization

The Heavy class can use small arms, but generally wields munitions launchers.

HUNTER

COVENANT MGALEKGOLO

Enormous in size and brutal in combat, the Lekgolo colony formation known as the Hunter is typically deployed as the Covenant's last resort in any given engagement. Hunters are usually encountered in pairs, one colony comprising two individual Hunters that are often called "bond brothers." These massive creatures are equipped with a powerful assault cannon and an enormous pavise shield, which is composed of the same material as the battleplate on the Covenant's immense capital ships. Hunters are unparalleled in size and strength within the Covenant, usually viewing other species as impeding irritations rather than allies, which often results in excessive collateral damage wherever they are deployed.

Spine orientation indicates temperament

Exposed Lekgolo gestalt reveals vulnerability

Fuel rod-based assault cannon

STATISTICS

AFFILIATION
Covenant

HOMEWORLD
Te

HEIGHT RANGE
12ft 1in–12ft 3in (368.7– 373.4cm)

WEIGHT RANGE
10,000–11,000lbs (4,536–4,990kg)

STATISTICS

AFFILIATION
Covenant

HOMEWORLD
Sanghelios

HEIGHT RANGE
7ft 4in–8ft 6in (223–259cm)

WEIGHT RANGE
307–393lbs (139–178kg)

STORM ELITE

COVENANT SANGHEILI

As the iron heart of the Covenant, the Sangheili have always been dominant in the alliance's military force, but now even more so than before. Most Covenant Sangheili fall within the Storm Elite class and, despite their substantial numbers, are still capable of leading smaller detachments of Unggoy and Kig-Yar. Generally speaking, a Storm Elite's armor is simple and sleek, yet it is more than competent for combat purposes. Unlike other Sangheili classes, Storm Elites are not specialized in one particular combat discipline or another, but can perform in assault roles, marksman roles, and even as scouts.

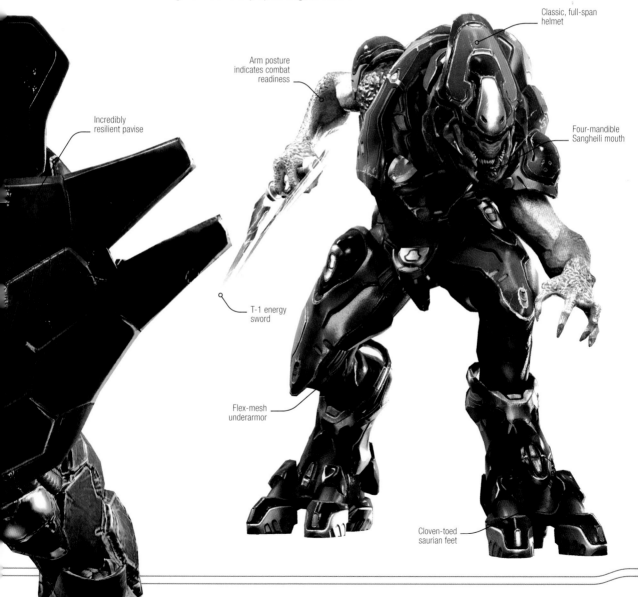

Classic, full-span helmet

Arm posture indicates combat readiness

Incredibly resilient pavise

Four-mandible Sangheili mouth

T-1 energy sword

Flex-mesh underarmor

Cloven-toed saurian feet

ELITE RANGER

COVENANT SANGHEILI

Elite Rangers are the Sangheili class dedicated to combat operations within exotic environments such as space, radioactive sites, and other hazardous locations that require the use of extra-vehicular activity equipment, modified armor, and gravity-mitigating thruster packs. Rangers operate similar to that of Storm Elites, though they are almost exclusively applied to EVA scenarios, such as ship-to-ship boarding actions or orbital assault and siege efforts. Unsurprisingly, Elite Rangers are also deployed to certain terrestrial sites that might benefit from gravity circumvention, life-sustaining atmospheric suits, or simply the ability to survive in hostile conditions.

Elite Rangers engaged the Master Chief in multiple environments on Requiem.

STATISTICS

AFFILIATION
Covenant

HOMEWORLD
Sanghelios

HEIGHT RANGE
7ft 4in–8ft 6in (223–259cm)

WEIGHT RANGE
307–393lbs (139–178kg)

Lightly armored harness

Forelimb thrust control

Hind-limb thrust control

Mesh suit extends shielding

Boots can magnetically latch if necessary

ELITE COMMANDER

COVENANT SANGHEILI

Seasoned and battle-hardened soldiers, Elite Commanders represent the Covenant's primary leadership in groundside engagements, generally ordering strategic direction to all Sangheili, Kig-Yar, and Unggoy combat squads in their command. The Sangheili who occupy this role have already served in the Covenant for decades, some on the ground and others on ships—and all of them have gained substantial experience, which has won them respect and power under Jul 'Mdama's new alliance. Most Elite Commanders utilize heavier, more elaborate armor sets displaying their heritage of skill and honor, while wielding their choice of marksman, explosive, and even guided-munitions weapons.

Commanders rarely engage without heavy firepower at their disposal.

Commander-class combat helmet

Interlocking under suit

Shield-negotiating cuisse

Predatory combat stance

High-frame greave system

Raised-claw reminiscent of ancient ceremonial armor

STATISTICS

AFFILIATION
Covenant

HOMEWORLD
Sanghelios

HEIGHT RANGE
7ft 4in–8ft 6in (223–259cm)

WEIGHT RANGE
307–393lbs (139–178kg)

ELITE WARRIOR

COVENANT SANGHEILI

Those who did not operate in a leadership capacity within the previous Covenant but demonstrated incredible skill are now allocated to the Elite Warrior class. During the war with the humans, such strength was determined by the number of lives taken—horrifically clear measures of triumph and victory. Sangheili in this class utilize powerfully reinforced combat harnesses and wield devastating explosive weapons like the Fuel Rod Cannon. Elite Warriors are one of the most intimidating Covenant classes in operation, known for suddenly and unexpectedly engaging enemies with devastating ferocity.

Accentuated helmet design

Shield-bolstering pauldron system

T-51 Carbine

Spaded cuisse

Ridge-locked lower greave

Warriors are rarely encountered in battle due to their comparatively low numbers.

STATISTICS

AFFILIATION
Covenant

HOMEWORLD
Sanghelios

HEIGHT RANGE
7ft 4in–8ft 6in (223–259cm)

WEIGHT RANGE
307–393lbs (139–178kg)

ELITE ZEALOT

COVENANT SANGHEILI

Without question the highest established of Covenant classes, Elite Zealots now represent both military and religious authority within the alliance, having taken all roles previously filled by the San'Shyuum. Historically, Zealots have been known for their ruthlessness and cruelty, even within the context of the Covenant. These characteristics are rivaled only by their cunning ability to track and eliminate targets. Although these Sangheili operate in a command capacity, they have not been spared from combat on the front lines—nor would they ever entertain such a notion: Zealots are still deployed to tenaciously hunt down their opponents, using the pinnacle of spec-ops tools and weaponry.

Fully shrouded helmet

Raised foil-arcs

Protective hand-armor

Organic, irregular armor surface native to Hesduros zealotry

Most of 'Mdama's Zealot class originated from the colony of Hesduros.

Traditional toe-claw common of Hesduros kaidons

STATISTICS

AFFILIATION
Covenant

HOMEWORLD
Sanghelios

HEIGHT RANGE
7ft 4in–8ft 6in (223–259cm)

WEIGHT RANGE
307–393lbs (139–178kg)

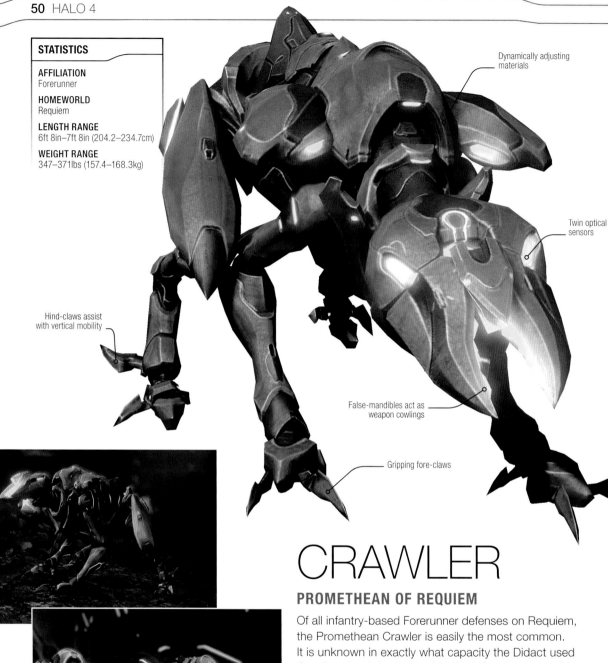

Dynamically adjusting materials

Twin optical sensors

Hind-claws assist with vertical mobility

False-mandibles act as weapon cowlings

Gripping fore-claws

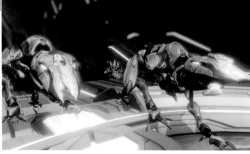

A Crawler's primary attacking mechanism is its head-mounted weaponry.

CRAWLER
PROMETHEAN OF REQUIEM

Of all infantry-based Forerunner defenses on Requiem, the Promethean Crawler is easily the most common. It is unknown in exactly what capacity the Didact used Crawlers, but it has been theorized that they were deployed deep into Flood redoubts to soften the parasite's infantry numbers before more valuable assets were sent in. Crawlers engage foes largely as pack hunters, collectively working together in close-knit groups to engulf and subdue enemies by way of sheer numbers and unrestricted ferocity. These predators can target enemies both near and far, and are even capable of vertically scaling structures in order to gain tactical advantage.

CRAWLER SNIPE

PROMETHEAN OF REQUIEM

Fielded for long-range combat and reconnaissance, the Crawler Snipe is a modified variant of the standard Crawler encountered on Requiem, designed specifically to track and kill from extreme distances. Apart from slight differences in size and shape, the Crawler Snipe's primary differentiator is its impressive use of Forerunner binary weapon technology, capable of quickly striking down enemies at range, disintegrating them with a single shot. These Crawlers are sent deep into enemy fronts, quickly seizing high vantage points from which they can cull out targets with unbelievable accuracy and devastating results. Doubtless, they are easily the most lethal element of the Crawler class.

STATISTICS
AFFILIATION Forerunner
HOMEWORLD Requiem
LENGTH RANGE 6ft 8in–7ft 8in (204.2–234.7cm)
WEIGHT RANGE 347–371lbs (157.4–168.3kg)

Supplemental energy stack

This Crawler Snipe is preparing to generate concentric targeting patterns around its head prior to firing.

Extreme-range sensor

Particle dilators

Fire-ready posture

ALPHA CRAWLER

PROMETHEAN OF REQUIEM

Chief among Promethean Crawlers is the Alpha Crawler, a commanding unit identified primarily by a series of hard light spikes lining its head and back. Alpha Crawlers are effectively pack leaders, guiding Crawler detachments of varying sizes into battle. Alphas are not always found within Crawler packs, and sometimes they appear in excess of three or four per pack. Nevertheless, they serve the same purpose within every context: to lead, augment, and fortify Crawler forces across the many environments of Requiem, providing vicious offensive capability up close and suppressive hard light firepower at range.

Alpha Crawlers are easily the most recognizable of their kind.

Spikes indicate status

Forelimb hints at dexterity

Mandibles cool and protect weapons

Lithe legs belie strength

High-pressure joint articulation allows explosive movement

STATISTICS

AFFILIATION
Forerunner

HOMEWORLD
Requiem

LENGTH RANGE
6ft 8in–7ft 8in (204.2–234.7cm)

WEIGHT RANGE
347–371lbs (157.4–168.3kg)

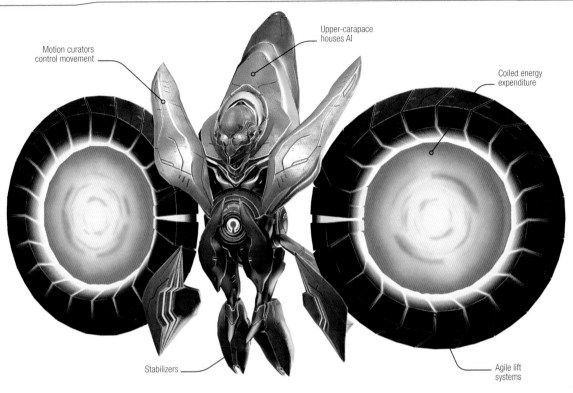

Motion curators
control movement

Upper-carapace
houses AI

Coiled energy
expenditure

Stabilizers

Agile lift
systems

WATCHER

PROMETHEAN OF REQUIEM

Requiem's primary defensive drones are called
Watchers, another creation of the Promethean
commander known as the Didact. These flying
machines are effectively low-level distributed
intelligences, Forerunner ancillas based on the Knight
they originate from. Watchers are initially held within
the armored shell of a Promethean Knight, but during
combat they emerge and take flight, providing
protection to their nearby allies from high above the
battlefield. Although much of their operation is
defensive, such as the
provision of energy
shielding, deflection of
explosives, and the
reconstitution of fallen
allies, they can also
operate offensively,
raining down fire on
enemies from above.

STATISTICS

AFFILIATION
Forerunner

HOMEWORLD
Requiem

HEIGHT
4ft 2in (127cm)

WEIGHT
318lbs (144.2kg)

The primary roles of a Watcher are surveying support and recon.

KNIGHT

PROMETHEAN OF REQUIEM

Designed and literally molded into existence by the Didact, Promethean Knights represent his final effort at destroying the Flood and preventing the firing of the Halo Array. These ancient and powerful warriors are not autonomous drones like Sentinels or even Crawlers, but are driven by the roiling vestiges of human essences composed during the final days of Forerunner history. Although their existence would not prevent the firing of Halo, they were tasked with guarding Requiem until the Didact was released. Now they do his bidding, preparing for war against the humans who the Didact ultimately blames for the destruction of his people.

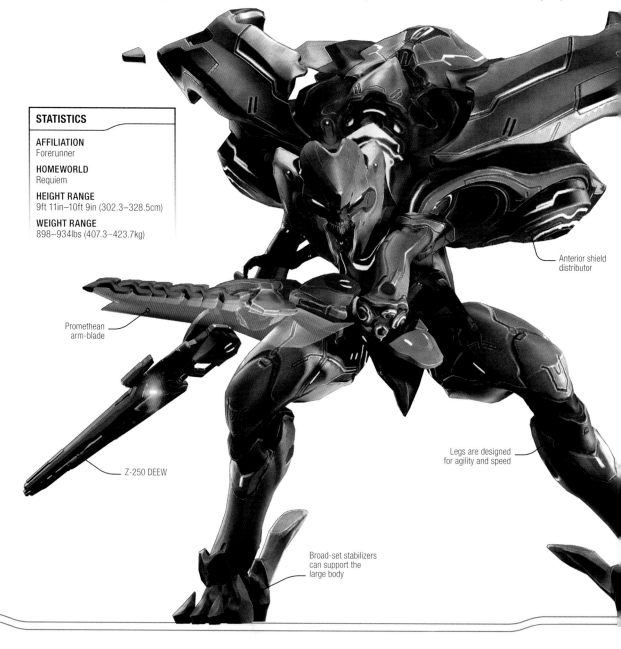

STATISTICS

AFFILIATION
Forerunner

HOMEWORLD
Requiem

HEIGHT RANGE
9ft 11in–10ft 9in (302.3–328.5cm)

WEIGHT RANGE
898–934lbs (407.3–423.7kg)

Anterior shield distributor

Promethean arm-blade

Z-250 DEEW

Legs are designed for agility and speed

Broad-set stabilizers can support the large body

Provides remote
sensory data

Transverse
sensor array

Pulse grenades
are generated
from arm joint

Extremely powerful legs

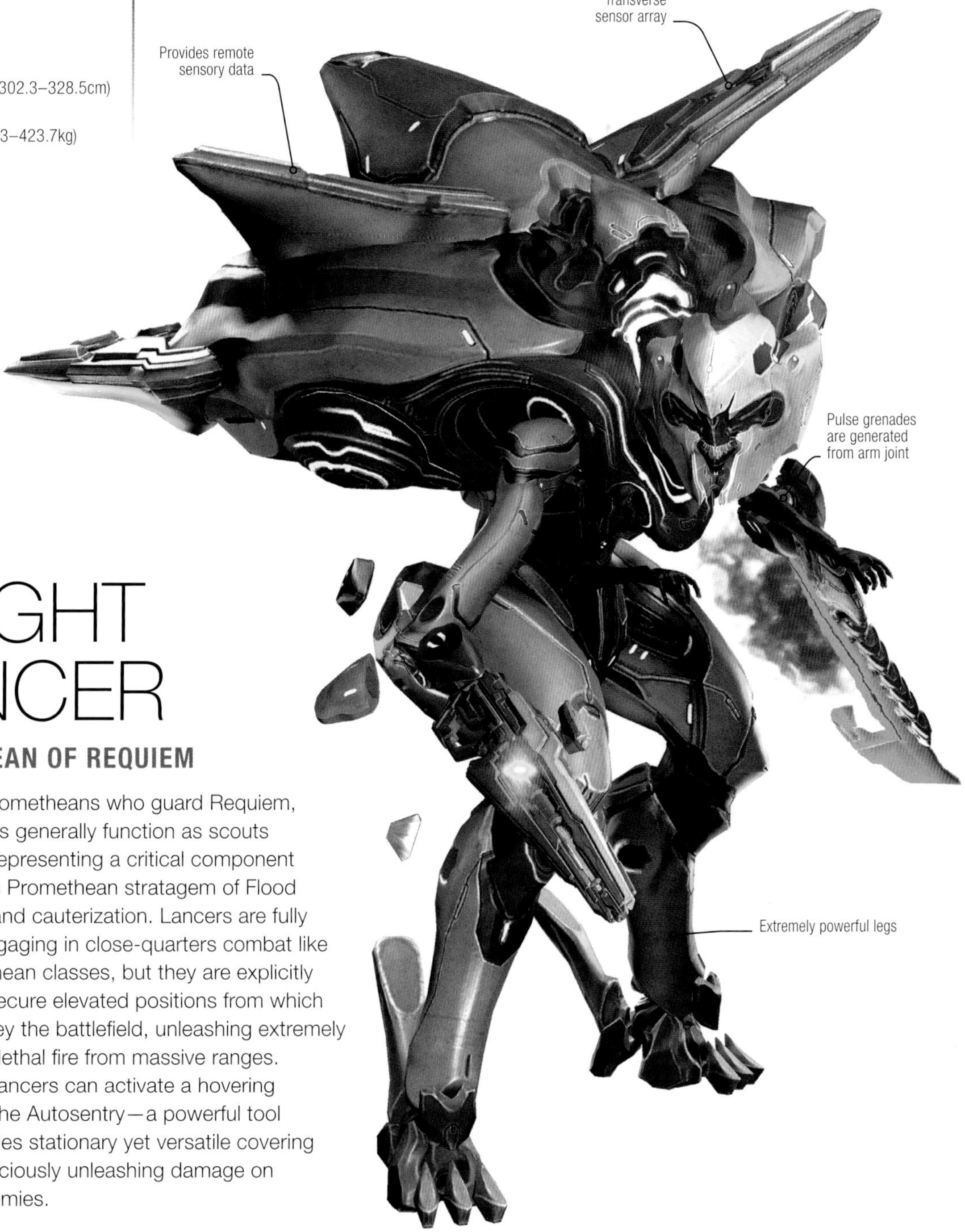

KNIGHT LANCER

PROMETHEAN OF REQUIEM

Among the Prometheans who guard Requiem, Knight Lancers generally function as scouts and snipers, representing a critical component in the Didact's Promethean stratagem of Flood containment and cauterization. Lancers are fully capable of engaging in close-quarters combat like other Promethean classes, but they are explicitly designed to secure elevated positions from which they can survey the battlefield, unleashing extremely accurate and lethal fire from massive ranges. Additionally, Lancers can activate a hovering drone called the Autosentry—a powerful tool that provides stationary yet versatile covering fire, tenaciously unleashing damage on any enemies.

AFFILIATION
Forerunner

HOMEWORLD
Requiem

HEIGHT RANGE
9ft 11in–10ft 9in (302.3–328.5cm)

WEIGHT RANGE
898–934lbs (407.3–423.7kg)

Light patterns
indicate command

Rippling light from
energy expenditure

Arm-blade is
composed of hard
light energy

KNIGHT COMMANDER

PROMETHEAN OF REQUIEM

Knight Commanders form the primary leadership of all Promethean Knight detachments, though this is a less rigid structuring based not on rate or experience, but rather on strategic necessity. Commanders are outfitted with impressively heavy armor and wield a powerful Forerunner weapon known as the Incineration Cannon—they are often deployed where substantial hostile forces exist. Knight Commanders are remarkable tacticians, but their use of incredible firepower, drone sentries, and enhanced vision make them formidable against large numbers of infantry, powerful weapon emplacements, or even heavy vehicles.

Reinforced joint offers fluid
movement despite size

Protrusions communicate rank

Excess energy discharge

Substantial resiliency in armor

Heavy-grade shield distributor

Z-250 DEEW

Counter-locking system for tactile balance

STATISTICS

AFFILIATION
Forerunner

HOMEWORLD
Requiem

HEIGHT RANGE
9ft 11in–12ft 2in (302.3–367.7cm)

WEIGHT RANGE
898–934lbs (407.3–423.7kg)

KNIGHT BATTLEWAGON

PROMETHEAN OF REQUIEM

Arguably the most dangerous and unpredictable of Promethean Knights, the creatures known as Knight Battlewagons are the most dominant force found on Requiem, created for close-quarters combat. Their hulking frames are covered in dense, resilient armor laced with fanned barbs of hard light. As their human-given name portends, the Knight Battlewagon is more of a walking weapon than an individual combatant. It is incredibly fierce in wielding the Promethean's classic Scattershot weapon as previously used during their war with the Flood. They are extraordinarily lethal and have been known to singlehandedly lay siege to even the most heavily fortified of sites.

WEAPONS

Assault Rifles are ideal for short- to mid-range combat scenarios such as urban warfare.

ASSAULT RIFLE

MA5D INDIVIDUAL COMBAT WEAPON SYSTEM

The Assault Rifle platform is the oldest rifle currently employed by the UNSC with production lines tracing back over two hundred years. Misriah Armory's ICWS (Individual Combat Weapon System) series has had more than a dozen models, its most pervasive being the MA5D ICWS. Like other Assault Rifles, the MA5D is an exceptionally resilient, gas-operated, magazine-fed, automatic rifle designed to execute close-quarters combat with lethal efficiency, regardless of hostile environmental conditions or duration of use in the field. The Assault Rifle's best feature is arguably its ruggedness and ability to withstand the challenging, frontier world conditions common to UNSC deployment.

STATISTICS

MANUFACTURER
Misriah Armory

AMMUNITION TYPE
M118 FMJ-AP

AMMUNITION SIZE
7.62 x 51mm

MAGAZINE CAPACITY
32 rounds

FIRING MODE
Automatic

LENGTH
39.2in (99.7cm)

WIDTH
3in (7.7cm)

HEIGHT
10.8in (27.4cm)

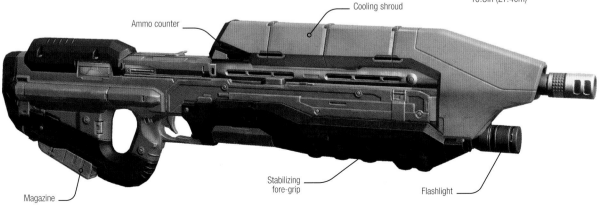

Ammo counter

Cooling shroud

Magazine

Stabilizing
fore-grip

Flashlight

BATTLE RIFLE

BR85 HEAVY-BARREL SERVICE RIFLE

Now commonplace in UNSC armories, contemporary Battle Rifles grew in popularity during the mid-2400s, just a few years prior to the Insurrection. Misriah's most current line of Battle Rifle is the BR85HB Service Rifle and it is widely considered their best model, particularly by the Marine Corps. The BR85 retains the BR55's gas-operated,

magazine-fed, semi-automatic design, optimized for three-round burst firing. The primary benefit that the Battle Rifle offers is that it adaptively maintains a solid set of ranges, with better close-range accuracy than most marksman rifles, but a substantially greater firing distance than the UNSC's mainline close-quarters assault weapons.

STATISTICS

MANUFACTURER
Misriah Armory

AMMUNITION TYPE
M634 X-HP-SAP

AMMUNITION SIZE
9.5 x 40mm

MAGAZINE CAPACITY
36 rounds

FIRING MODE
Semi-automatic, burst

LENGTH
39.1in (99.2cm)

WIDTH
2.4in (6.1cm)

HEIGHT
11.8in (29.9cm)

2x magnification sight

Misriah branded stock

Barrel

Stabilizing grip

Firing grip

The burst firing system is very effective against energy-shielded enemies.

The DMR deftly balances mid-range versatility with the ability to snipe from a distance.

Rear stock

3x magnification telescopic sight

Iron sight

Barrel

Magazine

Stabilizing fore-grip

Transportation clip

DMR

M395 DESIGNATED MARKSMAN RIFLE

The Designated Marksman Rifle (DMR) has been heavily favored by scouts and long-range marksmen for centuries. Although it saw some limited usage in certain branches during the introduction of Misriah's Battle Rifle, it is presently considered a favorite for mid- to long-range combat, offering tremendous stopping power over significant distances. Misriah Armory's leading model is the M395 DMR, a gas-operated magazine-fed rifle that maintains a smart-linked, telescopic, rail-mounted sight. Scout, Recon, and Pathfinder operators have uniformly preferred the DMR for its clean effectiveness and accuracy, even favoring it over Sniper Rifles for ease of use and transportability.

STATISTICS

MANUFACTURER
Misriah Armory

AMMUNITION TYPE
M118 FMJ-AP

AMMUNITION SIZE
7.62 x 51mm

MAGAZINE CAPACITY
14 rounds

FIRING MODE
Semi-automatic

LENGTH
46.9in (119.2cm)

WIDTH
2.9in (7.4cm)

HEIGHT
12.6in (32cm)

Cell-phasing meter

Aiming rail

M645 FTP-HE

Magnetic accelerator
channel

RAILGUN

ASYMMETRIC RECOILLESS CARBINE-920

Despite several variants being in full production for decades, Acheron Security's most recent attempt at Railgun weaponry is widely considered to be its best. The ARC-920 (Asymmetric Recoilless Carbine) is a compact-channel linear accelerator that fires a high-explosive round at incredible speed, simultaneously delivering kinetic and explosive force to targets of varying sizes and armor types. The Railgun's effectiveness is primarily based on accuracy, speed, and firepower, making it one of the most versatile explosive launchers ever incorporated into the UNSC armory. Although its usage against lightly armored vehicles is fairly obvious, many operators enjoy its vicious efficiency against heavily shielded enemy personnel.

STATISTICS	
MANUFACTURER	Acheron Security
AMMUNITION TYPE	M645 FTP-HE
AMMUNITION SIZE	16 x 65mm
MAGAZINE CAPACITY	1 round
FIRING MODE	Single-shot
LENGTH	43.6in (110.8cm)
WIDTH	2.9in (7.4cm)
HEIGHT	12.5in (31.7cm)

Due to their effectiveness against Covenant troops, many Spartans have incorporated rail weapons into their loadouts.

The smart-linked sight improves the overall accuracy of the M6 pistol.

MAGNUM

M6H PERSONAL DEFENSE WEAPON SYSTEM

Misriah Armory's most popular line of personal sidearms is unquestionably the M6 PDWS (Personal Defense Weapon System), which has been in production for roughly 150 years. Over those decades, the M6 has endured numerous, however slight, changes which have created several mainline variants favoring a myriad of combat roles and usages. Contemporarily, the M6H, a semi-automatic, recoil-operated, magazine-fed handgun, has led the field in post-war usage since 2555. The prominence of the M6 sidearm is quite remarkable, whether operating in a military capacity or in municipal police networks or even as a self-defense measure for civilians, all indicative of the high quality of this weapon.

Electroless nickel finish

2x magnification smart-linked sight

Modular LAM attachment

M9030 HEI/RD

Iron sight

Collapsible display

Safely switch

Firing grip

STICKY DETONATOR

M363 REMOTE PROJECTILE DETONATOR

Acheron Security, previously known for their domestic defense systems, has recently made claim to a variety of military-grade materiel lines after the loss of Chalybs Defense Solutions (CDS). One of the major areas of development has been in remote projectile detonators, where they have manufactured several series of explosive launchers. The M363 RPD is a low-profile, single-shot weapon that launches a magnetically latched explosive, which the operator can remotely detonate at a safe distance. Although previously manufactured in low quantities during the early part of the Insurrection, this weapon's size and ease-of-transportability has made it quite formidable, even during the war with the Covenant.

STATISTICS

MANUFACTURER
Acheron Security

AMMUNITION TYPE
M9030 HEI/RD

AMMUNITION SIZE
12.5cm

MAGAZINE CAPACITY
1 round

FIRING MODE
Single-shot

LENGTH
20.8in (52.9cm)

WIDTH
4.9in (12.5cm)

HEIGHT
9.9in (25.1cm)

Sticky Dets can offer users incredible strategic control when used properly.

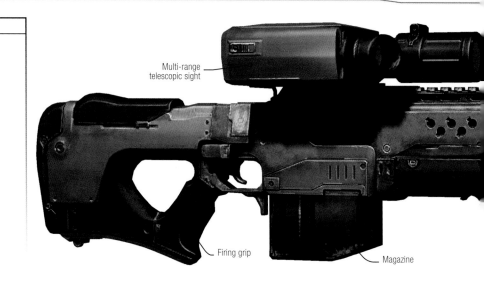

STATISTICS

MANUFACTURER
Misriah Armory

AMMUNITION TYPE
M232 APFSDS

AMMUNITION SIZE
14.5 x 114mm

MAGAZINE CAPACITY
4 rounds

FIRING MODE
Semi-automatic

LENGTH
63.5in (161.2cm)

WIDTH
8.7in (22cm)

HEIGHT
13.8in (35cm)

Multi-range telescopic sight

Firing grip

Magazine

SNIPER RIFLE

SNIPER RIFLE SYSTEM 99-SERIES 5 ANTI-MATERIEL

Unparalleled in long-range infantry combat, the UNSC's standard Sniper Rifle has been manufactured by Misriah Amory for over a hundred years. The most prominent of these is the SRS99 (Sniper Rifle System) series, which has proven its reliable performance and durability over decades of use. The weapon's dominance can be largely attributed to its overall effectiveness against the Covenant, even energy shielded enemies like the Sangheili, with its 14.5mm round easily capable of both buckling and penetrating energy shielding. In recent years, the Series 5 model has been the highest in production, heavily fielded in post-war combat operations and during classified military campaigns.

Heavy-gauge barrel

In the hands of an experienced marksman, the Sniper Rifle is an incredibly powerful tool.

Transportation handle

Heavy-gauge brace

Barrel

Bipod

STATISTICS

MANUFACTURER Misriah Armory	**FIRING MODE** Automatic
AMMUNITION TYPE M118 FMJ-AP	**LENGTH** 45.9in (116.5cm)
AMMUNITION SIZE 7.62 x 51mm	**WIDTH** 9in (22.8cm)
MAGAZINE CAPACITY 72 rounds	**HEIGHT** 12.3in (31.3cm)

Cooling shroud vent

Ammo meter readout

UNSC

Ammo drum

Firing grip

SAW

M739 LIGHT MACHINE GUN

During the 22nd century, SAWs (Squad Automatic Weapons) increased in usage, particularly during the first few major colonial conflicts. In response, Misriah Armory began to develop light machine guns that could serve in the SAW role, namely to support an entire squad, whether through suppressive fire or ammunition reserves. The most recent addition to this is the M739 LMG, a gas-operated, drum-fed, fully automatic machine gun that effectively provides sustained fire in the field, and is capable of suppressing even the most heavily armored of infantry targets. The M739, and a handful of its predecessors, saw increased usage throughout the late parts of the Insurrection and the Covenant War that followed.

The SAW is without equal among close-range fully automatic weapons.

ROCKET LAUNCHER

M41 SSR MEDIUM ANTI-VEHICLE/ASSAULT WEAPON

Surface-to-surface rocket launchers have been relatively common in infantry combat for hundreds of years, but they saw recent popularity during the Covenant War, where heavier firepower became a prerequisite against a superior foe. Without a doubt, Misriah Armory's most popular rocket launcher is the M41 SSR MAV/AW, a portable, twin-tube, shoulder-fired launcher capable of discharging 102mm rockets with impressive potential for destruction. Additionally, the M41 can designate rockets to home in on specific targets by tracking their heat signatures, making it particularly effective against airborne vehicles.

STATISTICS

MANUFACTURER
Misriah Armory

AMMUNITION TYPE
M19 SSM

AMMUNITION SIZE
102mm rocket

MAGAZINE CAPACITY
2 rockets

FIRING MODE
Semi-automatic

LENGTH
55.4in (140.6cm)

WIDTH
10.2in (25.9cm)

HEIGHT
17.4in (44.3cm)

2x magnification smart-linked sight

Transportation handle

Twin firing tubes

Stabilizing grip

Shoulder mount

SPNKR

Of all standard infantry anti-vehicle weapons, the Rocket Launcher remains the most powerful.

Smart-linked optics can assist
with kills over extreme ranges.

SPARTAN LASER

WEAPON/ANTI-VEHICLE M6 GRINDELL/ GALILEIAN NONLINEAR RIFLE

Relatively new to humanity's arsenal, infantry-held laser-firing weapons such as nonlinear rifles gained impressive notoriety during the Covenant War. Misriah Armory's attempt in this field was melded with a specific platform for a Mjolnir powered assault armor called GUNGNIR, an abbreviation of "Grindell/ Galileian Nonlinear Rifle," as both the armor and the weapon were optimized for each other. This eventually resulted in the colloquial name "Spartan Laser" for the M6 G/GNR, a shoulder-fired, smart-linked nonlinear rifle that projects a high-powered beam of energy. Although it is extremely proficient against vehicles, the Spartan Laser can be used against heavy infantry with remarkable precision.

STATISTICS	
MANUFACTURER	Misriah Armory
AMMUNITION TYPE	Series 6971 battery cell
AMMUNITION SIZE	N/A
MAGAZINE CAPACITY	4 shots
FIRING MODE	Semi-automatic
LENGTH	47in (119.3cm)
WIDTH	7.7in (19.5cm)
HEIGHT	15.4in (39.2cm)

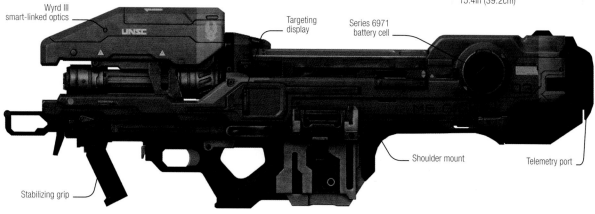

Wyrd III smart-linked optics

Targeting display

Series 6971 battery cell

Shoulder mount

Telemetry port

Stabilizing grip

At close-range, the Shotgun is brutally efficient against almost any enemy.

Barrel

Iron sight

Flashlight

Firing grip

Stock

SHOTGUN

M45D TACTICAL SHOTGUN

Despite often being considered antiquated within the context of 26th-century firearms, the shotgun has

The M45D is the most ubiquitous Misriah variant.

somehow managed to remain at the forefront of close-quarters infantry combat, possibly due to the emphasis on MOUT (Military Operations on Urban Terrain) and ship-to-ship boarding actions over the past few centuries. The most commonly encountered shotgun is currently Misriah Armory's M45D Tactical Shotgun, a pump-action weapon that fires 8-gauge cartridges with brutal proficiency. The M45D can provide swift and clean kills at close range, with a focus on infantry-grade breach and siege measures in tightly confined locations.

STATISTICS

MANUFACTURER
Misriah Armory

AMMUNITION TYPE
M296 TS

AMMUNITION SIZE
8 gauge

MAGAZINE CAPACITY
6 rounds

FIRING MODE
Semi-automatic

LENGTH
44.4in (112.9cm)

WIDTH
4.4in (11.2cm)

HEIGHT
9.6in (24.4cm)

MACHINE GUN

M247H HEAVY MACHINE GUN

Mounted turret emplacements are often deployed to defend UNSC-held territory or at specific chokepoints critical to local forces. The most commonly encountered UNSC turret is the rugged and powerful M247H Heavy Machine Gun (HMG) manufactured by Misriah Armory. The M247H HMG is an air-cooled, gas-operated, drum-fed automatic weapon, which is primarily used from a full-range, tripod-mounted position, providing powerful suppressive covering fire. Some operators have also been known to forcefully detach the weapon and carry it into battle, however these incidents are generally rare.

Placing the HMG at an elevated position is an optimal strategy.

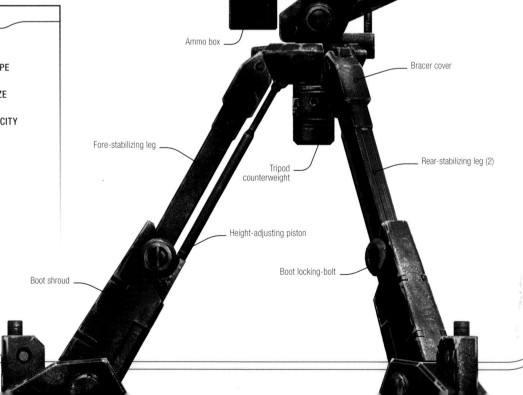

Sighting system

Gunner shield

Transportation handle

Ammo box

Bracer cover

Fore-stabilizing leg

Tripod counterweight

Rear-stabilizing leg (2)

Height-adjusting piston

Boot shroud

Boot locking-bolt

STATISTICS

MANUFACTURER
Misriah Armory

AMMUNITION TYPE
M340 HVE

AMMUNITION SIZE
12.7 x 99mm

MAGAZINE CAPACITY
200 rounds

FIRING MODE
Automatic

LENGTH
64.3in (163.4cm)

WIDTH
26.1in (66.4cm)

HEIGHT
25.3in (64.3cm)

STATISTICS

MANUFACTURER Misriah Armory	**FIRING MODE** N/A
AMMUNITION TYPE N/A	**LENGTH** 12in (30.5cm)
AMMUNITION SIZE N/A	**WIDTH** 7.2in (18.2cm)
MAGAZINE CAPACITY N/A	**HEIGHT** 18.9in (48.1cm)

The Chief used an H-295 FOM to assist *Infinity*'s forces in taking down key Particle Cannons above Requiem's surface.

TARGET DESIGNATOR

H-295 FORWARD OBSERVER MODULE

Employed most often by forward-positioned operators such as long-range scouts, force reconnaissance, and counter-intelligence personnel, target designators like Misriah Armory's H-295 FOM (Forward Observer Module) are critical to most major groundside campaigns. Leveraging an uplinked display and laser-painting systems, designators are almost always used to provide target acquisitions for fire support, which can include close-fire ground support, air strikes, and even orbital strikes from capital ships. The H-295 FOM can also be linked to specific vehicles, such as F-99 Wombat drones or even the UNSC's massive siegework platform, the M510 Mammoth, unleashing devastating firepower from a remote targeting link.

Module housing

Antenna transmitter

Module guard

Wedged mounting frame

Firing trigger

Handle

FOMs are ad hoc programmed in order to provide the most accurate intel for a given context.

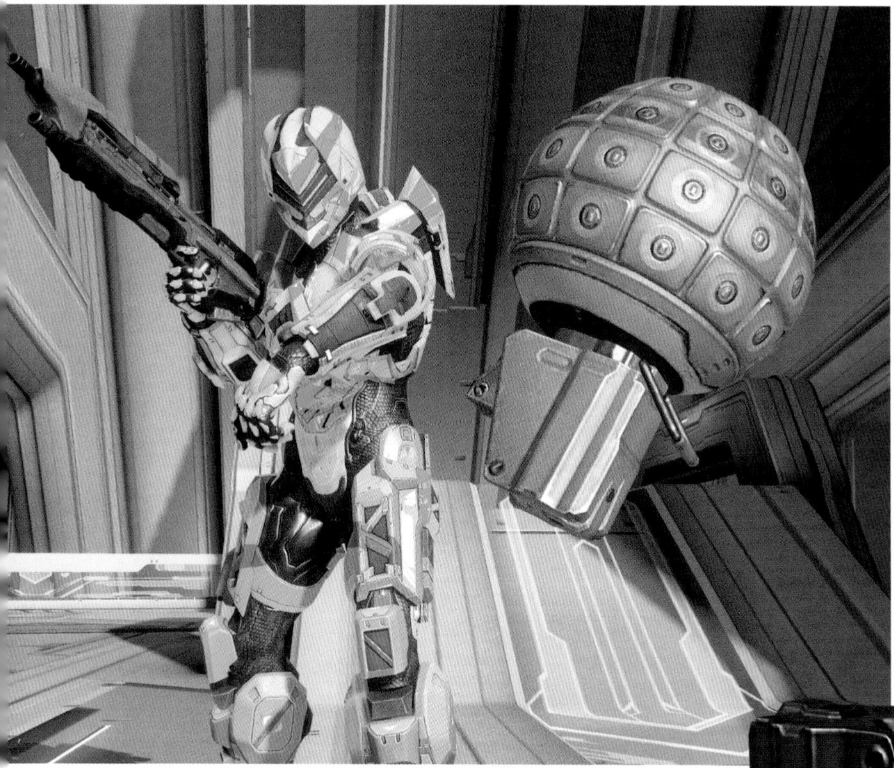

Frag grenades can often be scavenged from fallen allies.

FRAG GRENADE

M9 HIGH-EXPLOSIVE DUAL-PURPOSE ANTIPERSONNEL GRENADE

Fragmentation grenades are the most common type within the UNSC's explosives arsenal—a testament to their enduring quality across hundreds of years' worth of infantry combat. The M9 Fragmentation Grenade is a standard, high-explosive, dual-purpose grenade with a digital timer. It is extremely competent against personnel, particularly those who are dug-in or fixed behind cover because it can be ricocheted off hard surfaces. This effect, though surprisingly mundane, differentiates it from the Covenant's closest analog, the Plasma Grenade—essentially guaranteeing that this explosive's simplicity and efficiency will remain intact within the UNSC's arsenal for many years to come.

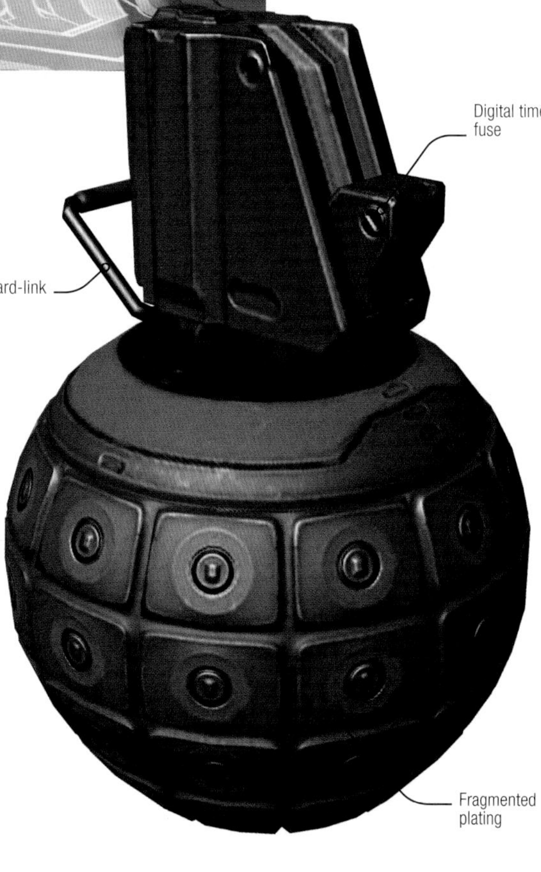

Digital timer fuse

BDU hard-link

Fragmented plating

Missile
nose

Supplemental
fuel line

Release port

Booster
base

HYPERION MISSILE

M4093 HYPERION NUCLEAR DELIVERY SYSTEM

Ship-based nuclear defense systems were first witnessed in space during the mid-22nd century, when interplanetary travel became pervasive. It wasn't until the early 2300s, however, that entire ship classes were being designed to this end, primarily due to concerns around colonial dissidence. Apart from a number of isolated incidents, for years nuclear force existed largely as a deterrent—until the arrival of the Covenant, when it then became a common tool of war. One of the most prominent of these weapons is the M4093 Hyperion Nuclear Delivery System—an external-accelerator launched, rocket-propelled missile developed by Acheron Security, now widely used on both frigates and destroyers.

STATISTICS

MANUFACTURER
Acheron Security

FILLER TYPE
Aeluphos-DTPF 9025

FILLER VOLUME
2.1 tons (1.9 tonnes)

LENGTH
202.6ft (61.7m)

WIDTH
51.9ft (15.8m)

HEIGHT
56.1ft (17.1m)

Hyperion missiles were designed for ship-to-ship naval warfare in space.

Forward Unto Dawn's Hyperion missile bay was still intact, despite its significant damage.

Infinity maintained a hull-mounted Onager in addition to its larger shipboard MACs.

Some automated Onagers actively protect stations such as Ivanoff from space debris.

ONAGER

MARK 2551/25CM PORTABLE - MAGNETIC ACCELERATOR CANNON

The term "Magnetic Accelerator Cannon" (MAC) refers to a general platform of large, linear-channel machines that generally fire a composited ferric-tungsten, depleted uranium round at supersonic speeds. While ship-mounted MACs are commonplace on any vessel with tonnage from frigate to carrier, most modular emplacements are low-profile mass drivers, such as

the Onager. Despite their immense size, these drivers are actually one of the smallest in their class, yet they are still remarkably efficient anti-ship weapons. Incredibly accurate and viciously powerful, emplacements like this launch their ultra-dense round deep into the target, irreparably crippling, if not outright obliterating it.

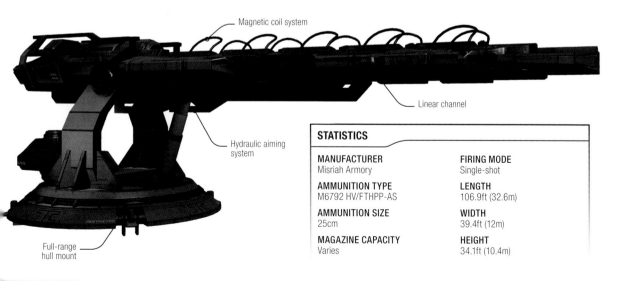

Magnetic coil system

Linear channel

Hydraulic aiming system

Full-range hull mount

STATISTICS

MANUFACTURER Misriah Armory	**FIRING MODE** Single-shot
AMMUNITION TYPE M6792 HV/FTHPP-AS	**LENGTH** 106.9ft (32.6m)
AMMUNITION SIZE 25cm	**WIDTH** 39.4ft (12m)
MAGAZINE CAPACITY Varies	**HEIGHT** 34.1ft (10.4m)

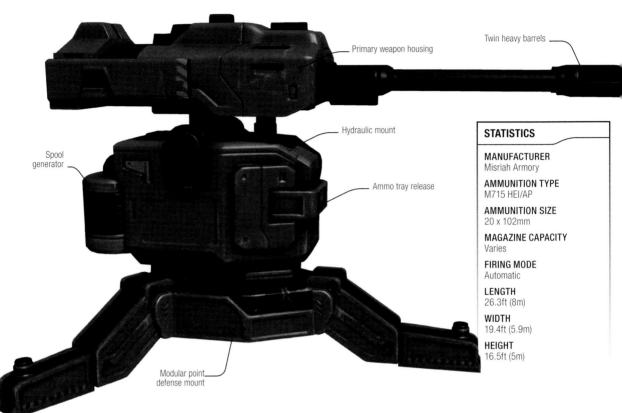

Primary weapon housing

Twin heavy barrels

Hydraulic mount

Spool generator

Ammo tray release

Modular point defense mount

STATISTICS

MANUFACTURER
Misriah Armory

AMMUNITION TYPE
M715 HEI/AP

AMMUNITION SIZE
20 x 102mm

MAGAZINE CAPACITY
Varies

FIRING MODE
Automatic

LENGTH
26.3ft (8m)

WIDTH
19.4ft (5.9m)

HEIGHT
16.5ft (5m)

SCYTHE

M85 ANTI-AIRCRAFT GUN

Often used at key locations within military bases and other heavily secured facilities, automated weapon emplacements come in a variety of sizes and designs and are typically controlled by a full-range sensor or artificial intelligence. The M85 Scythe is a low-profile, conveyor-fed, twin-barrel, anti-aircraft/ anti-spacecraft weapon manufactured by Misriah Armory. It is a variant typically fixed to orbital and suborbital military stations, as well as the exterior battleplate of ships when deemed necessary. Unlike the M71 Scythe, which was designed for terrestrial defense while in-atmosphere, the M85's fully sealed housing and nominal silhouette can be additionally used in space.

Despite *Infinity*'s enormous size and native armament, M85s were still used in its defense on Requiem.

Scythes are generally operated by remote actuators or dumb AIs.

LANCE

M97 GUIDED MISSILE WEAPON SYSTEM

Missile battery emplacements are easily the most effective means of anti-aircraft support, launching a bevy of high-explosive, self-guided missiles that actively home in on targets, providing impressive stopping power. The most popular of these is Misriah Armory's M97 Lance—a full-range, heavy-munitions, anti-ship artillery. It is not only competent within planetside engagements, but it is also optimized for combat in space. Much larger than the terrestrial M95, this enormous weapon emplacement can usually be found on the perimeter of critical space stations, elevator terminuses, and refitting anchors, as well as larger capital ships where mounting is deemed practical.

STATISTICS

MANUFACTURER
Misriah Armory

AMMUNITION TYPE
M4510 ASGM-7

AMMUNITION SIZE
85mm

MAGAZINE CAPACITY
Varies

FIRING MODE
Salvo

LENGTH
21.2ft (6.5m)

WIDTH
17.4ft (5.3m)

HEIGHT
18ft (5.5m)

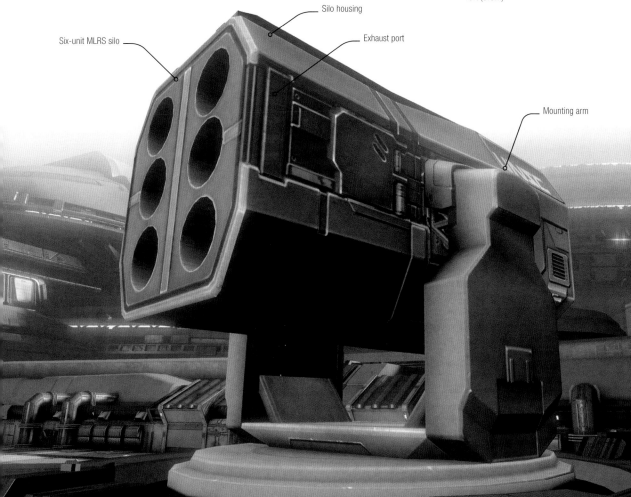

Six-unit MLRS silo

Silo housing

Exhaust port

Mounting arm

Infinity deployed a number of M97 emplacements to defend its hull from Covenant attackers.

VULCAN MACHINE GUN

M46 LIGHT ANTI-AIRCRAFT GUN

Without question, the most common armament of the Warthog platform is the Vulcan machine gun turret. Similar to the M41 mounted machine gun that came before it, the M46 Light Anti-Aircraft Gun continues the tradition of matching the Warthog's speed and mobility with a swift, lightweight, yet effective, firepower. Vulcan machine guns are usually employed against airborne enemies, as well as infantry and ground vehicles, by launching a barrage of 12.7mm rounds. Unlike other notable Warthog weapon emplacements, which require substantially more accuracy, the M46's spread and fully automatic nature provide more persistent firepower over a broader sector than any other.

Although generally found on Warthogs, Vulcans can be modularly fixed to other vehicles and structures.

STATISTICS

MANUFACTURER Misriah Armory	**FIRING MODE** Automatic
AMMUNITION TYPE M255 HVE rounds	**LENGTH** 109.8in (278.9cm)
AMMUNITION SIZE 12.7 x 99mm	**WIDTH** 39.4in (100cm)
MAGAZINE CAPACITY Varies	**HEIGHT** 76.7in (194.8cm)

Gunner shield

Targeting aperture

Iron sight

Triple barrel system

Barrel guard

Transportation grip

Shoulder brace

Firing grips

Belt-fed ammunition

Ammunition box

Warthog roll cage

ROCKET TURRET

M79 MULTIPLE LAUNCH ROCKET SYSTEM

STATISTICS

MANUFACTURER
Misriah Armory

AMMUNITION TYPE
M4510 ASGM-2

AMMUNITION SIZE
65mm

MAGAZINE CAPACITY
Varies

FIRING MODE
Salvo

LENGTH
74.9in (190.2cm)

WIDTH
77.2in (196.2cm)

HEIGHT
85.2in (216.4cm)

Undergoing a number of variants over the last several decades, the integrated rocket launcher emplacement has become a key fixture of heavy, mobile anti-aircraft support on the ground. The most conspicuous of these is the M79 Multiple Launch Rocket System, a hydraulically powered, full-range, twin-pod rocket launcher emplacement, which fires a cluster of six Argent V missiles near-simultaneously at a given target. This emplacement can be fixed to a number of vehicles and structures, but it is commonly featured on M12 Warthogs and the enormous M510 Mammoth, where it is used to fend off attacks from enemy aircraft, such as Banshees and Phantoms.

Each individual pod can fire three missiles in a single salvo.

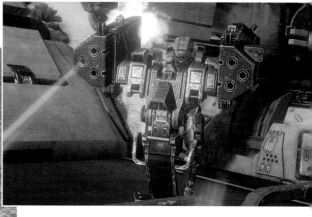

Two sensors allow coverage of both air and ground targets.

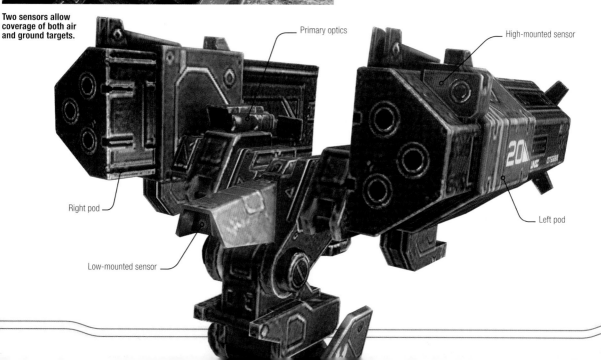

Primary optics

High-mounted sensor

Right pod

Low-mounted sensor

Left pod

GAUSS CANNON

M68 ASYNCHRONOUS LINEAR-INDUCTION MOTOR

The M68 Gauss Cannon is an extremely powerful weapon emplacement designed for anti-armor support, either in a fixed capacity or mounted on a vehicle. With its architecture having evolved over the years, the current variant of this weapon is optimized for use with vehicles such as the M12 Warthog, launching a viciously powerful tungsten-ferric round at supersonic speeds. Using an Asynchronous Linear-Induction Motor (ALIM) to leverage technology similar to that of magnetic accelerator cannons, Gauss Cannons are capable of punching holes into even the most resilient of armors, including that of Covenant Wraith tanks.

The Gauss Cannon generates incredible damage with minimal ammunition expenditure.

The M68's muzzle flash often attracts unwanted attention.

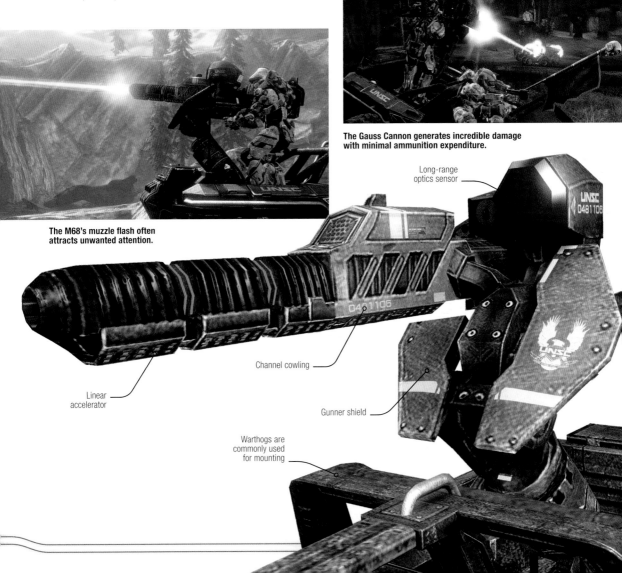

Long-range optics sensor

Channel cowling

Linear accelerator

Gunner shield

Warthogs are commonly used for mounting

FLANK GUN

M410 40MM DUAL HEAVY MACHINE GUNS/FLANK MOUNTED

Generally fixed to the main fuselage of Pelican gunships, bucket seat weapons such as these are designed to provide ground support coverage in the deployment and exfiltration of military personnel, as well as flanking lines of fire from the vehicle's blind spots. When mounted by Spartans, however, these weapons can be used to combat other aircraft high above a planet's surface and can even be employed in exoatmospheric scenarios, though for very specific uses. The M410 heavy machine gun fires 40mm gas-jacketed, depleted uranium rounds, tearing through infantry and vehicles, regardless of environmental conditions.

Mounting an M410 on a Pelican gunship is an extremely risky endeavor, as the operator is exposed and has no formal access back into the vehicle's bay.

STATISTICS

MANUFACTURER Misriah Armory	**FIRING MODE** Automatic
AMMUNITION TYPE M481 APGJDU	**LENGTH** 117.2in (297.7cm)
AMMUNITION SIZE 40mm	**WIDTH** 85.7in (217.6cm)
MAGAZINE CAPACITY Varies	**HEIGHT** 56.5in (143.4cm)

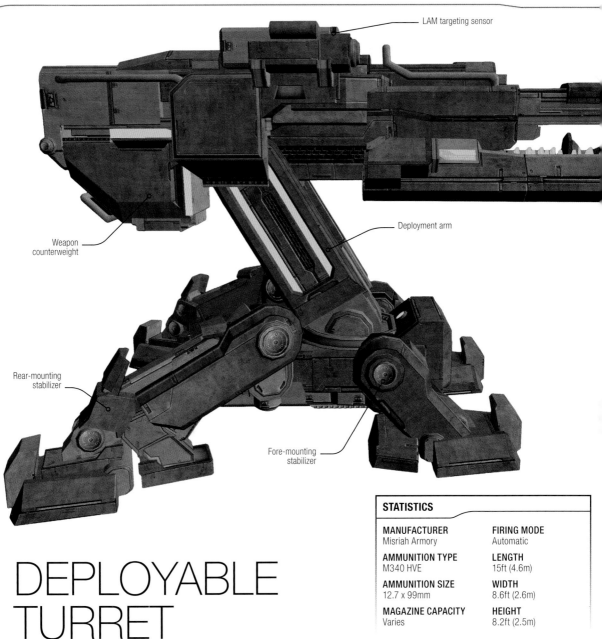

LAM targeting sensor

Weapon counterweight

Deployment arm

Rear-mounting stabilizer

Fore-mounting stabilizer

STATISTICS	
MANUFACTURER Misriah Armory	**FIRING MODE** Automatic
AMMUNITION TYPE M340 HVE	**LENGTH** 15ft (4.6m)
AMMUNITION SIZE 12.7 x 99mm	**WIDTH** 8.6ft (2.6m)
MAGAZINE CAPACITY Varies	**HEIGHT** 8.2ft (2.5m)

DEPLOYABLE TURRET

M3063 AUTOMATED HEAVY MACHINE GUN/SELF-TRACKING

Modular, extendable weapon emplacements that provide automated defense have become more common in recent years, particularly within remote operations where easily transportable emplacements help augment local forces. The M3063 Automated Heavy Machine Gun is a hydraulically mounted, full-range, self-tracking heavy weapon that fires

12.7mm rounds at any perceived enemy targets through a laser sensor and two stock-fixed linear cooling relays. Despite its ease of transport, this heavy weapon is most often used in a sentry capacity, positioned around high profile locations in order to provide immediate, ad hoc coverage against infantry and light vehicles when needed.

Barrel

Linear cooling system

HAVOK
NUCLEAR DEVICE

MARK 2556 MEDIUM FUSION DESTRUCTIVE DEVICE

Intriguingly, despite its incredibly destructive purpose, military-grade tactical nuclear devices are easily portable, coming in a variety of physical shapes and facilitating a number of functions. The most common design for these devices is a bare cylinder base with veiled key pad, typically seen with HAVOK, FURY, and FENRIS models. These machines, specifically referred to as MFDDs (Medium Fusion Destructive

Devices), are used as often for excavation and mining purposes as they are for warfare. In this frame, the device can either be latched to a rocket propulsion system for remote detonation or it can be detonated manually through the proper key sequence—the latter clearly implying that it would be a one-way trip for whoever triggered the device.

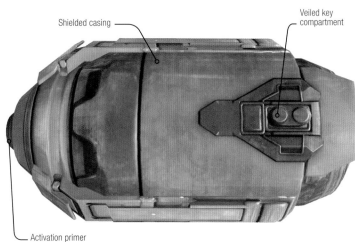

Shielded casing

Veiled key compartment

Activation primer

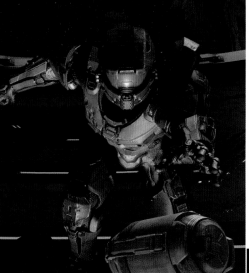

The Master Chief would use a Havok tactical nuke to stop the Didact.

MFDDs can be mounted onto Mjolnir hardpoints.

STATISTICS	
MANUFACTURER	Misriah Armory
FILLER TYPE	Mvalth-DTPF 80-S
FILLER VOLUME	31.4lbs (14.4kg)
LENGTH	13.8in (35cm)
WIDTH	7.1in (18cm)
HEIGHT	7.5in (19.1cm)

STATISTICS

MANUFACTURER
Iruiru Armory

AMMUNITION TYPE
Superheated Plasma

AMMUNITION SIZE
N/A

ENERGY CAPACITY
100 units

FIRING MODE
Semi-automatic

LENGTH
14.5in (36.9cm)

WIDTH
2.6in (6.6cm)

HEIGHT
11.8in (29.9cm)

PLASMA PISTOL

T-25 DIRECTED ENERGY PISTOL

Ubiquitous among Covenant soldiers of all ranks, the T-25 Plasma Pistol is the leading small arms of the alien collective. Despite its comparatively slight size, this weapon's discretion and versatility in combat is often favored above the more overpowered or fully automatic directed energy weapons. The pistol's main firing option is semi-automatic, short bursts of plasma, which can disable and kill soft targets, though it has little overall use against vehicles. What does affect vehicles is the pistol's scaled burst functionality, which overcharges the weapon's energy output, firing an EMP-like blast of plasma. This disabling effect is one of the most efficient anti-vehicle elements employed by Covenant soldiers.

Tracking sight

Holographic charge display

Upper-firing coil

Charging poles

Unggoy are generally armed with Plasma Pistols due to its discrete size and transportability.

Upper cowling

Exposed
crystalline shard

Channel brace

Firing grip

Stock/power supply

NEEDLER

T-33 GUIDED MUNITIONS LAUNCHER

Ballistic-based guided munitions launchers are rarely seen in the
Covenant, as the majority of their self-tracking launchers are based
on directed energy or superheated plasma. The T-33 Needler is an
exception to that rule. The single-handed, fully automatic launcher
fires shards of chemically charged crystals that were originally
discovered on the Sanghelios moon of Suban. When launched,
these shards home in on targets with astonishing speed and
persistence, usually impaling the target. Once enough have
hit their mark, the needles simultaneously explode through
proximal resonance instability, rendering the target
incapacitated. Despite conflicts on Sanghelios, most
mining sites on Suban continue to produce ammunition
for this exotic Covenant weapon.

STATISTICS

MANUFACTURER	**FIRING MODE**
Lodam Armory	Automatic
AMMUNITION TYPE	**LENGTH**
Crystalline Shards	28.8in (73cm)
AMMUNITION SIZE	**WIDTH**
4.8–6.3mm	8.5in (21.6cm)
MAGAZINE CAPACITY	**HEIGHT**
22 shards	20.9in (53cm)

Covenant weapons have become an integral part of the War Games.

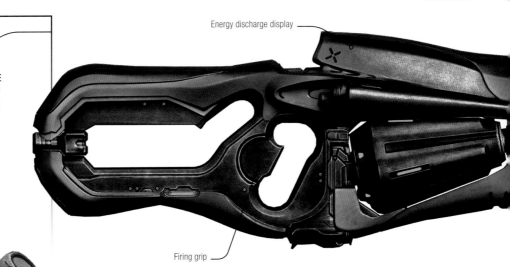

STATISTICS

MANUFACTURER
Lodam Armory

AMMUNITION TYPE
Superheated Plasma

AMMUNITION SIZE
N/A

ENERGY CAPACITY
100 units

FIRING MODE
Automatic

LENGTH
47.1in (119.6cm)

WIDTH
6in (15.4cm)

HEIGHT
12.2in (30.9cm)

Energy discharge display

Firing grip

Marksman barrel

STORM RIFLE

T-55 DIRECTED ENERGY RIFLE/ADVANCED

Based out of the industrial state of Lodam on the Sanghelios continent of Kaepra, Lodam Armory's first weapon in production was the T-55 Storm Rifle—a fully automatic assault rifle designed to replace the standard T-25 Plasma Rifle. Directed energy weapons are by far the most commonly used by the Covenant, known largely for their field resiliency, their ability to be easily recharged, and their overall effectiveness against both organic material and energy shielding. Lodam Armory claims that the Storm Rifle is greatly upgraded over its predecessor, with improvements to its coil set and cooling system as well as an elongated barrel to improve accuracy at range.

Even high-ranking Covenant wield the Storm Rifle.

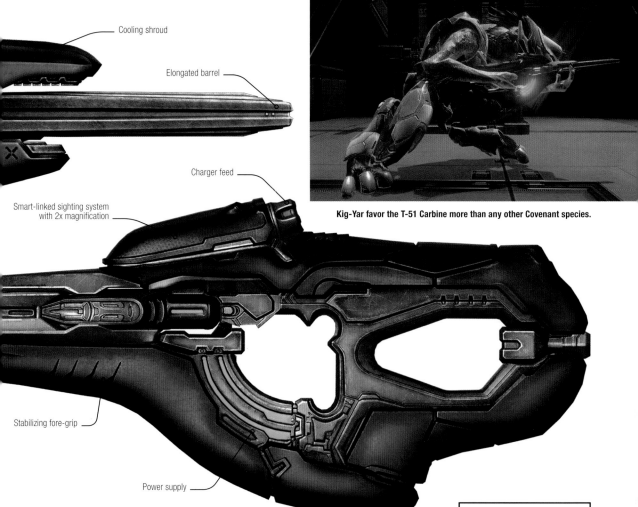

Cooling shroud

Elongated barrel

Charger feed

Smart-linked sighting system
with 2x magnification

Stabilizing fore-grip

Power supply

Kig-Yar favor the T-51 Carbine more than any other Covenant species.

COVENANT CARBINE

T-51 CARBINE

The T-51 Carbine is a remarkably compact marksman weapon employed by the Covenant. It is a recoil-operated, semi-automatic, charger-fed carbine. Rather than firing directed energy or superheated plasma, the carbine fires radioactively charged ballistic projectiles in a semi-automatic capacity. Despite its ammunition being similar in composition to that used by Fuel Rod Cannons, the T-51 Carbine's firing effect is intended to poison a target, expelling radioactively charged chemicals from a caseless round into the enemy's body. Generally speaking, the ballistic impact is usually enough to eliminate an enemy, but the carbine was designed to kill over time if impact was insufficient.

STATISTICS

MANUFACTURER
Iruiru Armory

AMMUNITION TYPE
Caseless Radioactive Round

AMMUNITION SIZE
8.7 x 60mm

MAGAZINE CAPACITY
18 rounds

FIRING MODE
Semi-automatic

LENGTH
52in (132.2cm)

WIDTH
6in (15.2cm)

HEIGHT
17.7in (44.9cm)

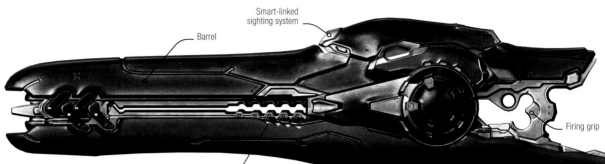

Smart-linked sighting system

Barrel

Firing grip

Accelerator channel

Coil set

BEAM RIFLE

T-27 SPECIAL APPLICATION SNIPER RIFLE

STATISTICS

MANUFACTURER
Merchants of Qikost

AMMUNITION TYPE
Ionized Particles

AMMUNITION SIZE
N/A

ENERGY CAPACITY
10 shots

FIRING MODE
Semi-automatic

LENGTH
69.3in (176cm)

WIDTH
10.1in (25.8cm)

HEIGHT
18.2in (46.1cm)

The Covenant utilize a number of long-range special application weapons used by scouts and designated marksmen. Currently, the most prominent of these is the T-27 Beam Rifle, an ion-based long rifle often seen in the hands of Kig-Yar snipers. The weapon ionizes hydrogen gas and launches charged particles through a linear accelerator at hypervelocity speeds. This incredibly fast beam carries impressive stopping power, capable of killing heavily armored infantry in one or two shots, depending on accuracy. Like other special application rifles used by the Covenant, the Beam Rifle sights targets via a smart-link system soft-patched into Kig-Yar and Sangheili helmets.

Mjolnir armor can patch into a Covenant weapon's smart-link system.

SHADE

T-55 ANTI-INFANTRY STATIONARY GUN

Based out of the Sanghelios continent of Tolvuus, Achoem Weapons continues the long-standing tradition of diversifying the Shade weapon emplacement. Like most Shade lines before it, the T-55 variant is used to quickly cut down infantry and secondarily to provide anti-air and anti-armor support against lighter vehicles when needed. While the physical shape of the Shade has evolved greatly, its basic function and purpose remain unchanged: It expels an unrelenting, fully automatic barrage of superheated plasma bolts, providing both direct and suppressive fire over reasonable distances, though with depreciating accuracy at greater ranges.

Unggoy are exceptional Shade operators.

STATISTICS

MANUFACTURER Achoem Weapons	**FIRING MODE** Automatic
AMMUNITION TYPE Superheated Plasma	**LENGTH** 14.9ft (4.5m)
AMMUNITION SIZE N/A	**WIDTH** 10.5ft (3.2m)
ENERGY CAPACITY Unlimited/Recycled	**HEIGHT** 8.5ft (2.6m)

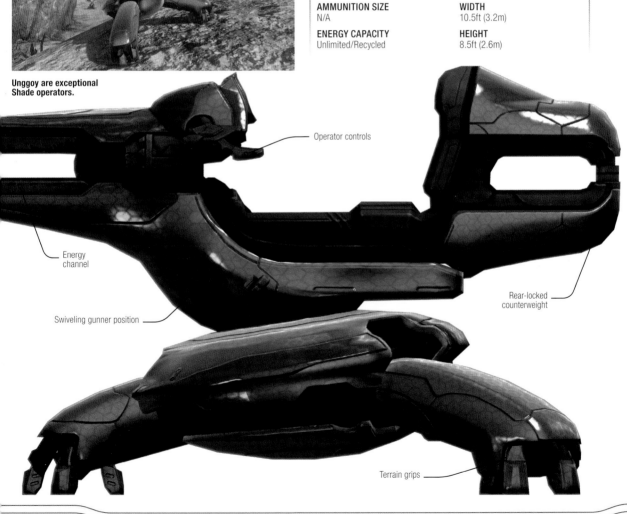

Operator controls

Energy channel

Swiveling gunner position

Rear-locked counterweight

Terrain grips

CONCUSSION RIFLE

T-50 DIRECTED ENERGY WEAPON/HEAVY

The T-50 Concussion Rifle is a close-range, anti-materiel munitions weapon often used against infantry and light vehicles. It fills a similar role to the human grenade launcher. Designed by the Sangheili's moon-based Merchants of Qikost, the Concussion Rifle charges mortar-like accretions of explosive plasma, similar to Wraiths and Revenants, firing them at enemy targets with relatively high speed and accuracy. While this is at a substantially lower grade than the heavy mortars used by vehicles, it is one of the more powerful weapons employed by infantry, capable of crushing even heavy infantry and overturning, if not outright destroying, enemy vehicles.

The Concussion Rifle is one of the Covenant's heaviest infantry weapons.

Expenditure display

Modular stock

Stabilizing fore-grip

Charger spindle

Firing grip

Sangheili Warriors often rely on the T-50 Concussion Rifle's explosive power.

STATISTICS

MANUFACTURER
Merchants of Qikost

AMMUNITION TYPE
Explosive Plasma

AMMUNITION SIZE
30mm

ENERGY CAPACITY
6 shots

FIRING MODE
Semi-automatic

LENGTH
40.5in (103cm)

WIDTH
7.1in (18cm)

HEIGHT
14.8in (37.6cm)

38mm fuel rods

Channel cowling

Shoulder mount

Firing grip

STATISTICS

MANUFACTURER
Merchants of Qikost

AMMUNITION TYPE
Fuel Rod

AMMUNITION SIZE
38mm

MAGAZINE CAPACITY
5 rounds

FIRING MODE
Semi-automatic

LENGTH
51.5in (130.8cm)

WIDTH
7.3in (18.5cm)

HEIGHT
21.6in (54.7cm)

FUEL ROD CANNON

T-33 LIGHT ANTI-ARMOR WEAPON

Usually carried by heavy weapon specialists in the field, the T-33 Fuel Rod Cannon is an incredibly powerful shoulder-mounted ballistic Covenant weapon that fires 38mm fuel rods, which violently explode upon impact. Although this weapon can be employed against infantry, it is generally considered gross overkill when used in that capacity, as its primary role is that of anti-armor and anti-materiel. The Fuel Rod Cannon has been so historically effective at this role that the same weapon technology has been incorporated into a number of Covenant vehicles, including the renowned T-26 Banshee and other ground support aircraft.

Extreme care is required during the operation of a Fuel Rod Cannon.

Some Spartans have been known to use Energy Swords in combat.

STATISTICS

MANUFACTURER
Merchants of Qikost

AMMUNITION TYPE
Shaped Plasma

AMMUNITION SIZE
N/A

ENERGY CAPACITY
100 units

FIRING MODE
N/A

LENGTH
50.6in (128.5cm)

WIDTH
9.5in (3.8cm)

HEIGHT
19.7in (50.1cm)

Razor-shaped plasma

Magnetic field generator

Hilt

ENERGY SWORD

T-1 ENERGY WEAPON/SWORD

The Covenant's T-1 Energy Sword is a weapon wielded by Sangheili for close-quarters, hand-to-hand combat, and has been historically regarded as an expression of a warrior's skill and honor. The blade's technology is simple though elegant, comprised of superheated plasma contained within and bound by magnetic lines that extend from the hilt, ultimately creating a lethal, razor-sharp martial weapon. For centuries, similar weapons, such as the curveblade and the twin-scythe, have defined the Sangheili's focus on physical combat, so the Covenant Energy Sword is viewed as the logical evolution of this cultural artifact.

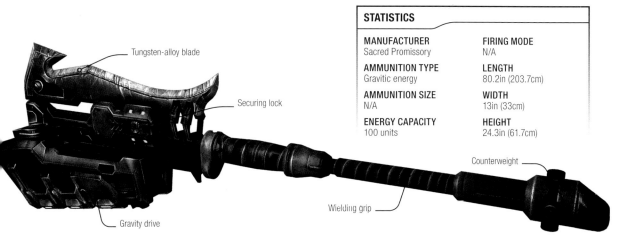

Tungsten-alloy blade

Securing lock

Gravity drive

Counterweight

Wielding grip

STATISTICS

MANUFACTURER	**FIRING MODE**
Sacred Promissory	N/A
AMMUNITION TYPE	**LENGTH**
Gravitic energy	80.2in (203.7cm)
AMMUNITION SIZE	**WIDTH**
N/A	13in (33cm)
ENERGY CAPACITY	**HEIGHT**
100 units	24.3in (61.7cm)

GRAVITY HAMMER

T-2 ENERGY WEAPON/HAMMER

With the relative lack of Jiralhanae exposure in the years since the war's end, the T-2 Gravity Hammer has been largely absent from the field. Designed as a part of the totemistic, clan-focused, patriarchal traditions of the Jiralhanae species, war hammers were often passed from one chieftain to another in an effort to maintain order within a given pack. With their integration into the Covenant, certain technologies were given to the Jiralhanae in order to enhance their weapon's and vehicle's performance, one of which was gravity-boosted magnetics. This hammer uses a shock-field generating gravity drive that increases damage on impact and can manipulate localized energy fields at the wielder's discretion.

A number of Gravity Hammers have been recovered from the field.

PLASMA CANNON

T-52 DIRECTED ENERGY SUPPORT WEAPON

The T-52 Plasma Cannon is a fully automatic directed-energy weapon mounted on a gravity-synched fulcrum tripod and used to fortify a given location. Unlike the heavier and larger Shade emplacement also employed by the Covenant, forcing an operator to fire from a vulnerable, stationary position, the Plasma Cannon can be removed from its mount and carried into combat if the operator is capable. This weapon's ease of transportability, its full targeting range, its energy shield cowling, and its exceptionally fast firing system make it an incredible asset in the field—particularly during defensive stands, where suppressive fire against encroaching enemies is a necessity.

STATISTICS

MANUFACTURER
Achoem Weapons

AMMUNITION TYPE
Superheated Plasma

AMMUNITION SIZE
N/A

ENERGY CAPACITY
200 units

FIRING MODE
Automatic

LENGTH
60.3in (153.2cm)

WIDTH
25.8in (65.5cm)

HEIGHT
33.8in (85.9cm)

Gunner shielding

Cell-cover plate

Modular cooling system

Controller frame

Gravity fulcrum

Emitter mount

Plasma Cannons can be fixed to the bay doors of a number of dropships.

The Plasma Grenade is possibly the most versatile and effective infantry explosive currently encountered in combat.

Priming button

Plasma release vent

Latent plasma filler

STATISTICS

MANUFACTURER
Iruiru Armory

FILLER TYPE
Latent Plasma

FILLER VOLUME
9.3oz (263.7g)

LENGTH
5.8in (14.6cm)

WIDTH
5.6n (14.2cm)

HEIGHT
6.1in (15.4cm)

PLASMA GRENADE

T-1 ANTIPERSONNEL GRENADE

The primary explosive used by the Covenant is the T-1 Plasma Grenade, developed and manufactured by the Iruiru Armory on Sanghelios. Despite its simplicity, the grenade's process and functionality are remarkable: After activation, the grenade becomes engulfed in latent plasma, a discharge that allows it to aggressively cling to specific heat or movement signatures before violently exploding on a timed fuse. While this grenade is extremely useful against infantry, it is even more so against vehicles, which are susceptible to the latent plasma due to their large, moving heat silhouette.

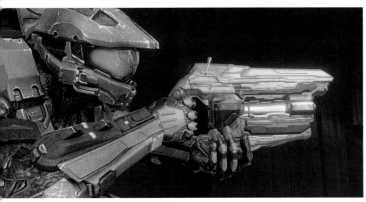

Boltshots are surprisingly powerful when used accurately.

Light mass channel

STATISTICS

MANUFACTURER
Unknown/Forerunner Origin

AMMUNITION TYPE
Ionized Particles

AMMUNITION SIZE
N/A

ENERGY CAPACITY
10 units

FIRING MODE
Semi-automatic

LENGTH
21.3in (54.1cm)

WIDTH
3.7in (9.4cm)

HEIGHT
12.5in (31.8cm)

BOLTSHOT

Z-110 DIRECTED ENERGY PISTOL/EXOTIC

Although variants of this technology existed earlier, the Z-110 Boltshot came to prominence approximately two hundred years before the firing of the Halo Array, a full century into the Forerunners' bloody war against the Flood. The Boltshot is a close-range particle dilator created to optimize precision-based infantry combat against organic tissue, such as the FSC (Flood Super Cell) material which comprises the Flood parasite. One unique attribute of this weapon is its burst-firing action, which releases an overloaded dispersal of ionized particles—an astonishingly powerful blast that is devastating to enemy infantry.

Indicator mounting brace

Strength dilator

Particle emitter

Overload conduction plates

Energy cell bay

Spectrum sensor

Exhaust plate

Strength dilator

Minor expenditure cell

Major expenditure cell

SUPPRESSOR

Z-130 DIRECTED ENERGY AUTOMATIC WEAPON

First introduced by the Forerunners during the Kradal conflicts, the Z-130 Suppressor was an impressive fully automatic infantry weapon that grew in standing during the war with the humans and the Flood conflict that followed thousands of years later. Utilizing a classic coil set architecture that the Covenant would later reverse engineer for many of their weapons, the Suppressor charges bolts of hard light energy, dispersing them at steeply increasing speeds. The effect is impressively accurate at close-range and would often be used during rare ship boarding actions, where Forerunners intended to seize vessels previously held by the Flood.

STATISTICS	
MANUFACTURER Unknown/Forerunner Origin	**FIRING MODE** Automatic
AMMUNITION TYPE Light Mass	**LENGTH** 37.1in (94.2cm)
AMMUNITION SIZE N/A	**WIDTH** 5.9in (15cm)
ENERGY CAPACITY 48 units	**HEIGHT** 14.2in (36cm)

Suppressors ruthlessly breach personal energy shields when fired accurately.

Easily the most lethal close-range weapon encountered by humans.

SCATTERSHOT

Z-180 CLOSE COMBAT RIFLE/ASYMMETRIC ENGAGEMENT MITIGATOR

The Z-180 Scattershot saw a great deal of action in the hands of Builder Security battling the Flood during large scale evacuation efforts held across the Forerunner ecumene. While most Forerunner infantry managed to battle the parasite at a distance, in rare cases some were forced to engage the enemy up close—and it was in this context that the Scattershot channel weapon excelled beyond most others in its class. Many security teams leveraged the Scattershot's impressive schismatic dispersal effect as they purged infected cities, allowing the weapon's particle beams to strategically ricochet off any nearby hard surfaces, essentially creating a cauterizing grid of lethal energy within some environments.

STATISTICS	
MANUFACTURER	Unknown/Forerunner Origin
AMMUNITION TYPE	Ionized Particles
AMMUNITION SIZE	N/A
MAGAZINE CAPACITY	5 units
FIRING MODE	Semi-automatic
LENGTH	45.5in (115.5cm)
WIDTH	4.2in (10.7cm)
HEIGHT	13.4in (34.1cm)

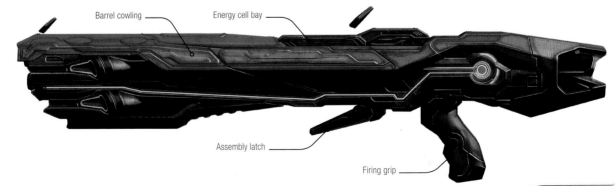

Barrel cowling — Energy cell bay —

Assembly latch —

Firing grip —

LIGHTRIFLE

Z-250 DIRECTED ENERGY ENGAGEMENT WEAPON

The Z-250 LightRifle was pioneered during the ground campaigns of the human war. It was originally designed to achieve precision-based sniping with light mass componential particle acceleration. LightRifles such as this one use a diffused combination of particle acceleration and hardened photonic matter to fire extremely fast and accurate beams, capable of dropping most individual enemies in just a few well-placed shots. Warrior-Servant marksmen used these during large-scale siege efforts against ancient human redoubts, as this particular weapon served well against the opposition's numerous particle rifles.

STATISTICS	
MANUFACTURER	Unknown/Forerunner Origin
AMMUNITION TYPE	Light Mass
AMMUNITION SIZE	N/A
ENERGY CAPACITY	36 units
FIRING MODE	Semi-automatic
LENGTH	49.5in (125.7cm)
WIDTH	4in (10.1cm)
HEIGHT	12.6in (32cm)

Integrated targeting optics

Stock

Firing grip

Stabilizing fore-grip

Light mass channel

When zoomed-in on a target, the LightRifle burst fires three units at a time.

BINARY RIFLE

Z-750 SPECIAL APPLICATION SNIPER RIFLE

Yet another example of the Forerunners' incredible mastery over technology—and more specifically, brutally destructive technology—the Binary Rifle was designed early in Forerunner history, though the current Z-750 model was only introduced late in their civilization in order to contend with the Flood. Using the power of twin, core-mounted particle accelerators, the Binary Rifle has the ability to neutralize most infantry types, even those of considerable mass, by jacketing antimatter particles within a charged beam, which effectively annihilate the target's composition upon impact. Rifles such as this became critically necessary when dealing with a variety of large Flood "pure forms" that were encountered in parasite-controlled sites.

STATISTICS	
MANUFACTURER	Unknown/Forerunner Origin
AMMUNITION TYPE	Ionized Particles
AMMUNITION SIZE	N/A
ENERGY CAPACITY	2 units
FIRING MODE	Semi-automatic
LENGTH	75in (190.5cm)
WIDTH	5in (12.6cm)
HEIGHT	15.6in (39.5cm)

Extreme-range integrated optics

Stock

Firing grip

Expenditure release

Though challenging to aim at close-range, the effect is still quite devastating.

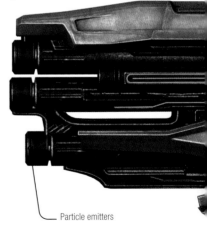

Particle emitters

INCINERATION CANNON

WEAPON/ANTI-MATERIEL Z-390 HIGH-EXPLOSIVE MUNITIONS RIFLE

Often used to strategically purge sites rapidly undergoing transformation into Flood control, the Z-390 Incineration Cannon is a shoulder-mounted munitions launcher that fires a high concentration of explosive particles along multiple, undulating streams. As brutally destructive as such cannons are, their place in the Forerunner arsenal is a rather delicate one. Prometheans used this specific weapon when assaulting any location believed to hold a Gravemind, or even early-forming spore mountains, where Forerunner command deemed that the infestation too small to invoke ship weapons, but far too large to be dealt with via traditional infantry arms.

Knight's wielding Incineration Cannons are incredibly formidable.

The Z-390 appears to bury antimatter within undulating particle streams, horrifically dismantling physical composition upon impact.

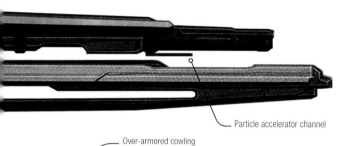

Particle accelerator channel

Over-armored cowling

Release vent

Firing grip

STATISTICS

MANUFACTURER Unknown/Forerunner Origin	**FIRING MODE** Burst
AMMUNITION TYPE Ionized Particles	**LENGTH** 53.1in (134.8cm)
AMMUNITION SIZE N/A	**WIDTH** 7.9in (20cm)
ENERGY CAPACITY 1 unit	**HEIGHT** 15.9in (40.5cm)

Pulse Grenades can be extremely useful in close-quarters.

PULSE GRENADE

Z-040 ATTENUATION FIELD GENERATOR/LOCALIZED

During the Flood's Coordinated Stage, when the parasite has had sufficient room to gather, organize, and grow, it creates vast strongholds composed of resilient FSC (Flood Super Cell) accretions, quickly developing a Gravemind and becoming truly lethal. The Z-040 Pulse Grenade and all adjacent attenuation technologies were employed by Forerunners for the purpose of cauterizing enemy-held sites such as these. Generally speaking, the Pulse Grenade is a field-generating explosive that can actively damage any targets that persist within its ionization radius, before violently collapsing and disintegrating nearly all organic material types within its sphere.

STATISTICS

MANUFACTURER
Unknown/Forerunner Origin

FILLER TYPE
Ionization Pulse

FILLER VOLUME
N/A

LENGTH
5.6in (14.2cm)

WIDTH
5.6in (14.2cm)

HEIGHT
5.6in (14.2cm)

Ionization fields are maintained for just a short time before suddenly and violently collapsing.

Catching prong

Designed to generate spherical field

Field exerting node

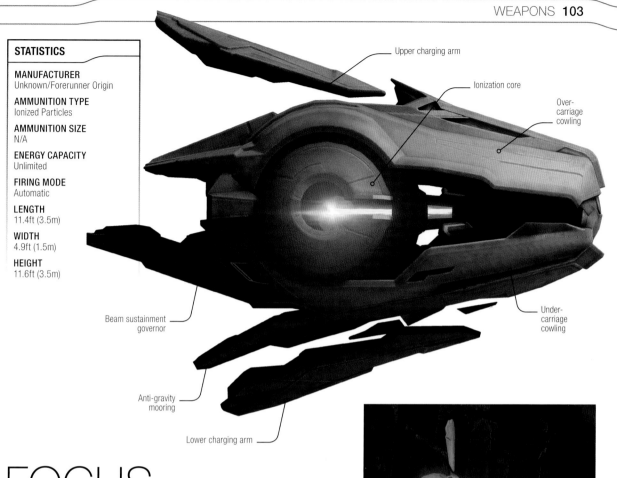

STATISTICS

MANUFACTURER
Unknown/Forerunner Origin

AMMUNITION TYPE
Ionized Particles

AMMUNITION SIZE
N/A

ENERGY CAPACITY
Unlimited

FIRING MODE
Automatic

LENGTH
11.4ft (3.5m)

WIDTH
4.9ft (1.5m)

HEIGHT
11.6ft (3.5m)

Upper charging arm

Ionization core

Over-
carriage
cowling

Under-
carriage
cowling

Beam sustainment
governor

Anti-gravity
mooring

Lower charging arm

FOCUS TURRET

Z-510 DIRECTED ENERGY FOCUS WEAPON

Encountered across the surface of Requiem and on a number of other Forerunner worlds, the Z-510 Focus Turret is a versatile defensive weapon emplacement capable of being instantaneously phased into an environment at key strategic points in order to provide defensive and suppressive lines of fire. While these Focus Turrets can economically use ion particle arrays like many other Forerunners weapons, the Covenant would later attempt to reverse-engineer this technology using comparatively primitive electromagnetically guided plasma with weapons like the T-52 Focus Rifle. Nevertheless, focused particle acceleration remains an unbelievably strong localized weapon type.

The Focus Turret preempts attack by splaying its charging arms.

This weapon's operation and effect is extremely similar to that of the Sentinel Beam.

Ionization core

Upper channels

HEAVY ARTILLERY

Lower channel

FORERUNNER ARTILLERY

Z-8250 ANTI-SHIP EXTERIOR DEFENSE NETWORK

No strangers to planetary and space warfare, the Forerunners manufactured thousands of different anti-ship weapons, all of which greatly surpass humanity's current technological capacity. The most notable of these were likely the installed artillery encountered on Requiem and the Didact's enormous ship, *Mantle's Approach*. What little can be gleaned from the scans and reports collected is that they were composed of both physical materials and sustained energy, together supplying a pivot point, power modulation, and ammunition. This artillery can operate individually, but it is most often used within a complex network and guarding other larger weapons in a support capacity, such as the Forerunners' immense, defensive particle cannons.

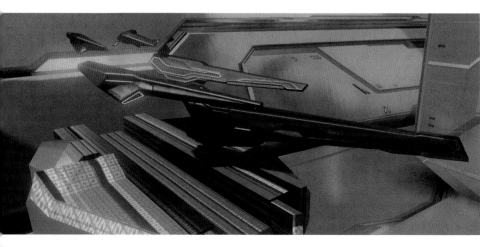

LIGHT ARTILLERY

STATISTICS

MANUFACTURER
Unknown/Forerunner Origin

AMMUNITION TYPE
Ionized Particles

AMMUNITION SIZE
N/A

ENERGY CAPACITY
Unlimited

FIRING MODE
Automatic

LIGHT ARTILERY LENGTH
237.4ft (72.4m)

LIGHT ARTILERY WIDTH
121.7ft (37.1m)

LIGHT ARTILERY HEIGHT
85.3ft (26m)

HEAVY ARTILERY LENGTH
251.7ft (76.7m)

HEAVY ARTILERY WIDTH
82.4ft (25.1m)

HEAVY ARTILERY HEIGHT
71.7ft (21.9m)

Forerunner artillery networks are generally controlled by response actuators or low-order ancillas.

PARTICLE CANNON

Z-8060 HIGH-IMPACT PARTICLE WEAPON

The enormous Z-8060 Particle Cannons are probably one of the most powerful scaled weapons that the Forerunners employ. They guard both Requiem and the Didact's enormous warship, *Mantle's Approach*, and are capable of visiting absolute devastation on approaching enemy vessels. Both accurate and extraordinarily powerful, Particle Cannons launch a hyper-dense collection of negatively charged ions, a roiling super-heated composite that can rip through large enemy ships in a single salvo. Though not always the case, some Particle Cannons are protected by much smaller anti-ship emplacements, positioned to guard the cannons' ion reactors, as well as provide constant suppressive fire.

STATISTICS	
MANUFACTURER	Unknown/Forerunner Origin
AMMUNITION TYPE	Ionized Particles
AMMUNITION SIZE	N/A
ENERGY CAPACITY	Unlimited
FIRING MODE	Single-shot
LENGTH	1,606.7ft (489.7m)
WIDTH	1,051.4ft (320.5m)
HEIGHT	910.5ft (277.5m)

UNSC *Infinity* was pinned down by Requiem's powerful Particle Cannons for some time.

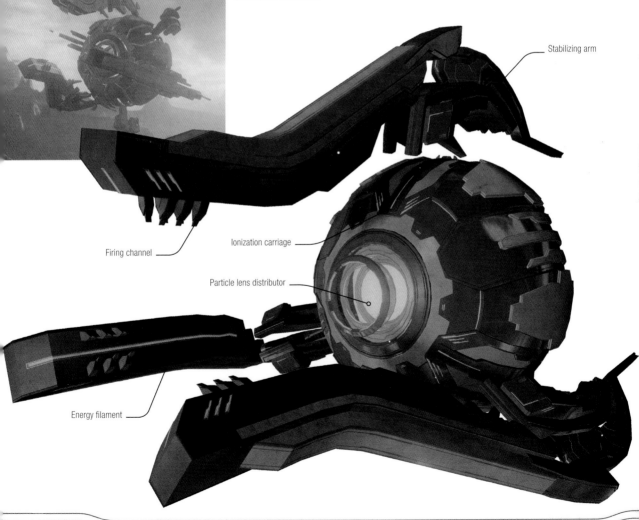

Stabilizing arm

Firing channel

Ionization carriage

Particle lens distributor

Energy filament

VEHICLES

WARTHOG

M12 FORCE APPLICATION VEHICLE

The reason for the M12 Warthog's prominence is without a doubt the vehicle's rich versatility. In addition to its light composite armor and its impressive maneuverability, the M12 Warthog can support a wide range of personnel transportation and weapon emplacement needs, adding significantly to its practical application. These features, coupled with a rugged, in-field resiliency have maintained the Warthog's renowned legacy for decades. The vehicle's most common variant is easily the M12 LRV (Light Reconnaissance Vehicle), which features a pneumatically powered, 360-degree range M46 Vulcan Light Anti-Aircraft Gun, primarily designed for use against aircraft and infantry.

Warthogs balance excellent firepower with impressive maneuverability on rough terrain.

Gunner controls

M46 LAAG

Roll cage

12.0L liquid-cooled hydrogen-injected ICE

UNSC

Driver's controls

Towing winch

All-terrain, heavy-grade tires

STATISTICS

MANUFACTURER AMG Transport Dynamics	**LENGTH** 20.5ft (6.3m)
CREW CAPACITY 3 personnel	**WIDTH** 9.8ft (3m)
PRIMARY ARMAMENT M46 Vulcan LAAG	**HEIGHT** 8.1ft (2.5m)

MONGOOSE

M274 ULTRA-LIGHT ALL-TERRAIN VEHICLE

AMG Transport Dynamics began manufacturing light-armored ATVs in 2483 and have since generated seventeen versions of the impressive Mongoose. Their most recent edition is the M274 Ultra-Light All-Terrain Vehicle, which is used almost exclusively for the transportation of personnel and materiel. The primary benefit of the Mongoose against other ATVs and LRVs is not speed, but rather maneuverability and optimized control over difficult terrain and challenging environmental conditions. Common practice among Spartans, though not advised by UNSC safety protocols, is the use of an armed, rear-loaded passenger, effectively weaponizing the Mongoose.

STATISTICS

MANUFACTURER
AMG Transport Dynamics

CREW CAPACITY
2 personnel

PRIMARY ARMAMENT
N/A

LENGTH
10.6ft (3.2m)

WIDTH
6.1ft (1.8m)

HEIGHT
4.9ft (1.5m)

Side mirror

Rear-loading mount

Driver's stirrups

Heavy-gauge suspension cage

High-traction tread

Although made for utility, the Mongoose has also been involved in combat.

In the field, Spartans often push the M274 to its absolute limits.

Although dangerous, personnel can ride the M808's tracks and provide anti-infantry support.

STATISTICS

MANUFACTURER
Acheron Security

CREW CAPACITY
6 personnel

PRIMARY ARMAMENT
M512 90mm SBHVC

SECONDARY ARMAMEMNT
M247 MMG

LENGTH
33.6ft (10.2m)

WIDTH
25.5ft (7.8m)

HEIGHT
14.5ft (4.4m)

SCORPION

M808 MAIN BATTLE TANK

The most widely known main battle tank utilized by the UNSC, the M808 Scorpion was originally developed by the Meridian-based Chalybs Defense Solutions group. This contract was sadly lost in the flames of the Covenant's razing of the colony. After the close of the war, Acheron Security, a defense contractor based on Mars, took over production of the classic design, only slightly modifying it. Scorpions are both resilient and mobile, equipped with a powerful primary cannon that can fire devastating 90mm rounds and a medium machine gun, which supplies effective mid-range anti-infantry suppression.

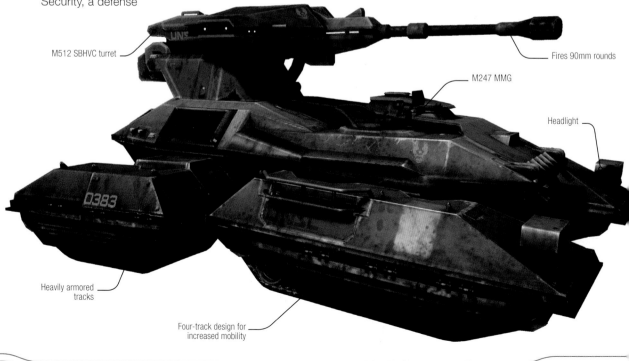

M512 SBHVC turret

Fires 90mm rounds

M247 MMG

Headlight

Heavily armored tracks

Four-track design for increased mobility

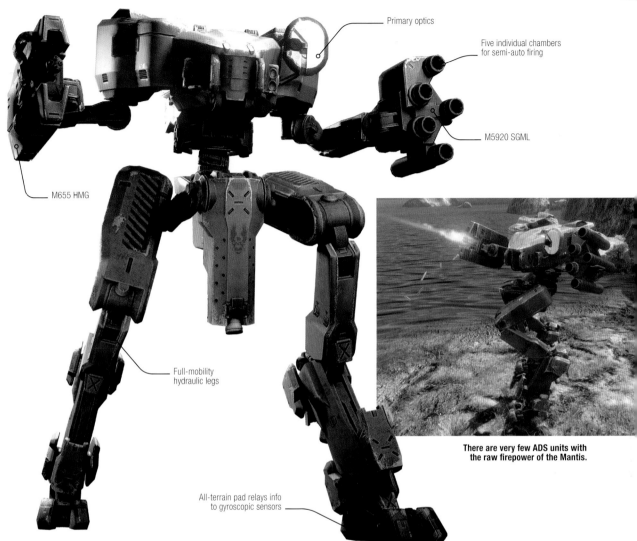

Primary optics

Five individual chambers
for semi-auto firing

M5920 SGML

M655 HMG

Full-mobility
hydraulic legs

All-terrain pad relays info
to gyroscopic sensors

**There are very few ADS units with
the raw firepower of the Mantis.**

MANTIS

HRUNTING/YGGDRASIL MARK IX ARMOR DEFENSE SYSTEM

The Mark IX ADS (Armor Defense
System) is the product of decades' worth
of both technological development and
functional iteration, eventually culminating
in a human machine without physical
equal. Leveraging a powerful ultra-heavy
four-barrel machine gun on one arm
and a multi-chamber high-explosives
munitions launcher on the other, the
Mantis is the UNSC's most effectively

versatile single-operator ground vehicle.
The Mark IX is referred to as the Mantis
likely due to its ability to ambush
enemies, without warning and across a
variety of terrains, or possibly because
of the legendary "Cherbourg Run" said
to have been conducted by the first
prototype against eighteen heavily
guarded T-27 AACs during the Battle
of Meridian.

STATISTICS	
MANUFACTURER	Materials Group
CREW CAPACITY	1 operator
PRIMARY ARMAMFNT	M655 20mm HMG/AM
SECONDARY ARMAMEMNT	M5920 35mm SGML/AM
LENGTH	9.3ft (2.8m)
WIDTH	19ft (5.8m)
HEIGHT	18.6ft (5.7m)

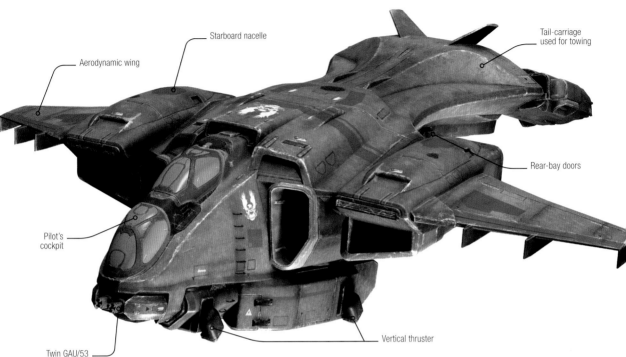

Aerodynamic wing

Starboard nacelle

Tail-carriage
used for towing

Rear-bay doors

Pilot's
cockpit

Twin GAU/53
MBHRC

Vertical thruster

PELICAN DROPSHIP

DROPSHIP 79 HEAVY-TROOP CARRIER

For several decades, the Pelican dropship has been the UNSC's best and most prominent method of troop and materiel transportation both terrestrially, in-atmosphere, and exoatmospherically across localized space. Misriah Armory's contemporary D79 variant has seen the most substantial post-war usage, differentiating itself from the D77 and D78 variants by way of its increased armor, separated operator stations, twin nose-mounted rotary cannons, and impressive weapon modularity (which has led to the heavily armed G79 variant). Although the UNSC retains a healthy fleet of dropships including the D82 Darter and the D96 Albatross, the Pelican's primacy remains unchallenged.

STATISTICS	
MANUFACTURER Misriah Armory	**LENGTH** 100.6ft (30.7m)
CREW CAPACITY 15–20 personnel	**WIDTH** 82.7ft (25.2m)
PRIMARY ARMAMENT GAU/53 70mm MBHRC (2)	**HEIGHT** 35.2ft (10.7m)

The D79 is the primary dropship of the UNSC *Infinity*.

PELICAN GUNSHIP

GUNSHIP 79 HEAVY-TROOP CARRIER/MOBILE ARMORY

Since its inception, the Pelican has long been considered by many to be a heavily armed gunship capable of actively engaging in combat, so the G79 Heavy-Troop Carrier/Mobile Armory is simply a formalization of the dropship's robust versatility, but with improvements to weaponry. Not only does this variant utilize its fuselage as a mobile armory (bearing exposed weapon caches), but it also leverages an M8 Laser Cannon alongside a standard rotary cannon and two flanking machine gun buckets. Some versions of this Pelican have even included a heavy topside cannon, similar to the one used by light battle tanks.

STATISTICS

MANUFACTURER
Misriah Armory

CREW CAPACITY
15-20 personnel

PRIMARY ARMAMENT
H GAU/53 70mm MBHRC / M8C G/GNC

SECONDARY ARMAMEMNT
M369 90mm SBHVC/DM

TERTIARY ARMAMENT
M410 40mm DHMG/FM (2)

LENGTH
100.6ft (30.7m)

WIDTH
82.7ft (25.2m)

HEIGHT
35.2ft (10.7m)

With its extraordinary arsenal, the G79 has few alien counterparts within the Covenant.

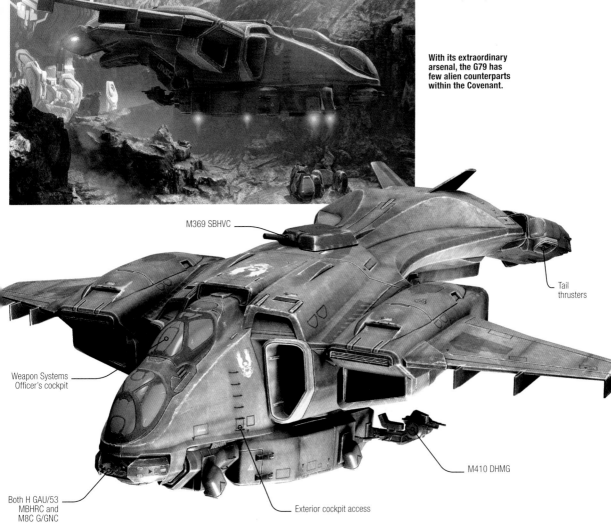

M369 SBHVC

Tail thrusters

Weapon Systems Officer's cockpit

M410 DHMG

Both H GAU/53 MBHRC and M8C G/GNC

Exterior cockpit access

BROADSWORD

F-41 EXOATMOSPHERIC MULTI-ROLE STRIKE FIGHTER

Hailing from the same production line as the GA-TL1 Longsword and the B-65 Shortsword, the F-41 Broadsword is Misriah Armory's solution for cross-environmental, multi-role fighter combat, utilized most often by the UNSC Air Force to engage in suborbital dogfights. The Broadsword has been in production for more than two decades, though it only saw prominence toward the end of the war. Despite the F-41's primary arsenal being its twin 35mm autocannons and its pair of Medusa missile pods, the fighter can also be under slung with nuclear pacification materiel, making it not only a remarkable combat vehicle, but also an excellent ordnance delivery system.

STATISTICS

MANUFACTURER
Misriah Armory

CREW CAPACITY
1 operator

PRIMARY ARMAMENT
M1075 ASW/AC 35mm MLA

SECONDARY ARMAMEMNT
M6088 ST/Medusa MP

LENGTH
66.3ft (20.2m)

WIDTH
64.5ft (19.7m)

HEIGHT
35.7ft (10.9m)

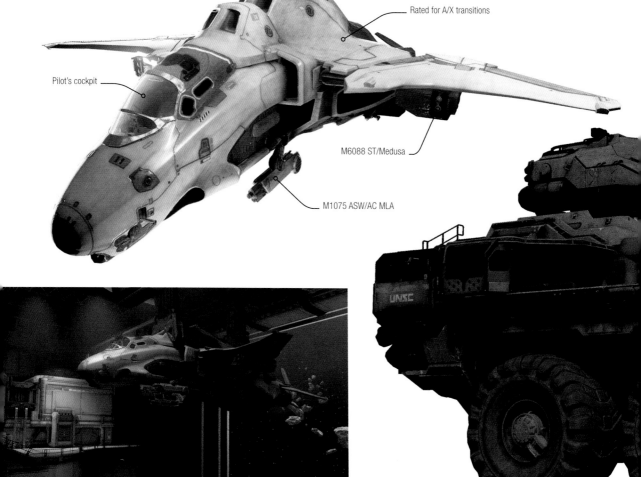

Rated for A/X transitions

Pilot's cockpit

M6088 ST/Medusa

M1075 ASW/AC MLA

Ivanoff maintained at least three Broadswords on-site at all times.

MAMMOTH

MOBILE ANTI-AIRCRAFT WEAPONS PLATFORM
M510 SIEGEWORK/ULTRA-HEAVY

By any standard, the M510 Mammoth siegework is the largest and most powerful terrestrial vehicle currently used by the UNSC, tactically operating as a mobile forward operating and assault base. Greatly exceeding the size and firepower of the M312 and M313 Elephants, the Mammoth's purpose is not limited to convoy support or asset recovery, but is often focused on direct assault or blockade, utilizing an exceptionally powerful heavy rail gun and several emplacement mounts that are typically occupied by rocket launcher turrets. Despite these impressive characteristics, the Mammoth's lack of speed and dexterity requires a complement of personnel and vehicles for localized defense.

STATISTICS

MANUFACTURER Acheron Security	**LENGTH** 224.2ft (68.3m)
CREW CAPACITY 30-35 personnel	**WIDTH** 107.6ft (32.8m)
PRIMARY ARMAMENT Mark 2547/35cm HRG	**HEIGHT** 89ft (27.1m)
SECONDARY ARMAMEMNT M79 65mm MLRS (2)	

The M510 often deploys other vehicles from within.

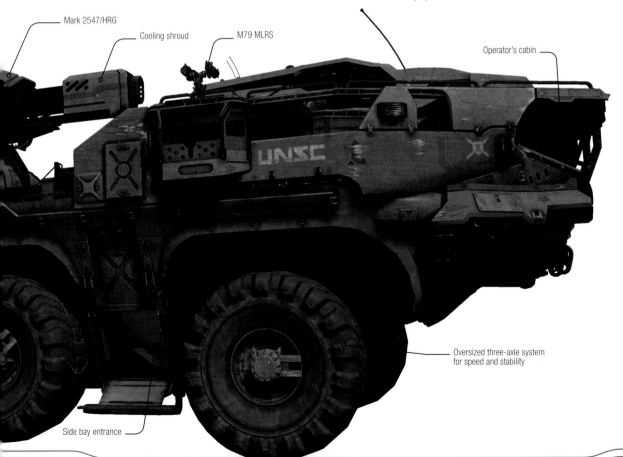

Mark 2547/HRG

Cooling shroud

M79 MLRS

Operator's cabin

UNSC

Oversized three-axle system for speed and stability

Side bay entrance

Operator's seat

Exposed drive line

Operator's stirrup

T-32 DEW/L

GHOST

T-32 RAPID ATTACK VEHICLE

The T-32 Ghost's long and established history within the Covenant clearly boasts the success of its operational viability and the ubiquity of its use. As a single-manned assault vehicle, the Ghost is largely unmatched. Its remarkable mobility, excellent speed, and effective firepower are only offset by the open cockpit, which obviously places the operator at risk. The Covenant use the Ghost primarily as a scouting or reconnaissance vehicle, sending it behind enemy lines to track and monitor an adversary's movement. It can also be used to engage enemies with reasonably large infantry numbers and even well-armed, light vehicles.

Control valence

STATISTICS

MANUFACTURER	LENGTH
Iruiru Armory	13.8ft (4.2m)
CREW CAPACITY	**WIDTH**
1 operator	12.6ft (3.9m)
PRIMARY ARMAMENT	**HEIGHT**
T-32 DEW/L (2)	6ft (1.8m)

Ghosts are deployed in coordination with each other to improve combat efficiency.

WRAITH

T-26 ASSAULT GUN CARRIAGE

An aggressively armored and highly mobile mortar tank, the Covenant's T-26 Wraith was created specifically to besiege enemy positions with unrelenting firepower, while maintaining a relatively safe position. This effect is realized through the Wraith's primary weapon, a heavy mortar, which can launch explosive plasma high into the air before violently cascading down onto enemies at significant distances. The Wraith's mobility source is its boosted gravity drive, a powerful system that offers reasonable agility despite its substantial size, and can also swiftly boost forward with impressive speed.

STATISTICS

MANUFACTURER
Lodam Armory

CREW CAPACITY
2 personnel

PRIMARY ARMAMENT
T-26 35cm DEM

SECONDARY ARMAMEMNT
T-26 DEWE

LENGTH
29ft (8.8m)

WIDTH
30.1ft (9.2m)

HEIGHT
12.3ft (3.8m)

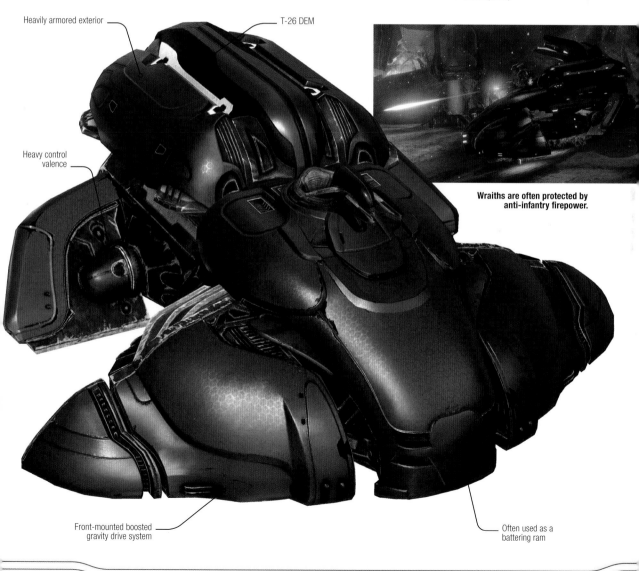

Heavily armored exterior

T-26 DEM

Heavy control valence

Wraiths are often protected by anti-infantry firepower.

Front-mounted boosted gravity drive system

Often used as a battering ram

PHANTOM

T-44 TROOP CARRIER

Interestingly, the newly formed Covenant that follow Jul 'Mdama have been encountered using the T-44 Phantom, an earlier variant of the heavily armored line of Covenant dropships, leaving some to speculate that these were the most available after the war. There is little difference between this vehicle and its derivatives, aside from its armor's remarkable resiliency and a number of operational features. The Phantom's appeal has been largely attributed to its exceptional speed and maneuverability across the full spectrum of environmental conditions, both atmospheric and exoatmospheric. These ingredients, alongside a reasonable volume of firepower, make it a formidable dropship with very few shortcomings.

T-44 Phantoms can be equipped with lateral boarding chutes to deploy troops in confined spaces where the larger T-28 boarding craft are not suited.

STATISTICS

MANUFACTURER Achoem Weapons	**SECONDARY ARMAMEMNT** T-52 DESW (2)
CREW CAPACITY 25 personnel	**LENGTH** 109ft (33.2m)
PRIMARY ARMAMENT T-44 DEW/M	**WIDTH** 65.9ft (20.1m)
	HEIGHT 41.2ft (12.6m)

Side bay door

Heavily armored exterior

Materiel gravity anchors

Anti-gravity lift

Utilizes impulse drive for space travel

Stabilizer valence

BANSHEE

T-26 GROUND SUPPORT AIRCRAFT

Easily one of the most recognizable of Covenant vehicles, the T-26 Banshee continues to operate as their fundamental ground support aircraft. Lithe, highly maneuverable, and armed with a pair of twin-linked Plasma Cannons and a heavy Fuel Rod Cannon, the Banshee is a remarkable tool in groundside engagements. Post-war modifications have allowed the standard vehicle to be deployed in a limited scouting capacity within space, but its most effective usage is in a terrestrial capacity, providing nimble, heavily armed overwatch support for groundside forces, with the ability to swoop down and destroy enemies at will.

STATISTICS	
MANUFACTURER	Lodam Armory
CREW CAPACITY	1 operator
PRIMARY ARMAMENT	T-26 DEW/L
SECONDARY ARMAMEMNT	T-26 HAAW/M
LENGTH	23.2ft (7.1m)
WIDTH	24.7ft (7.5m)
HEIGHT	11.7ft (3.6m)

Aerodynamic contours

Armored canopy

Control valence

Canard aileron

T-26 DEW/L

Pilot's cockpit

T-44 DEW/M

Banshees can swiftly boost over short distances to evade enemies.

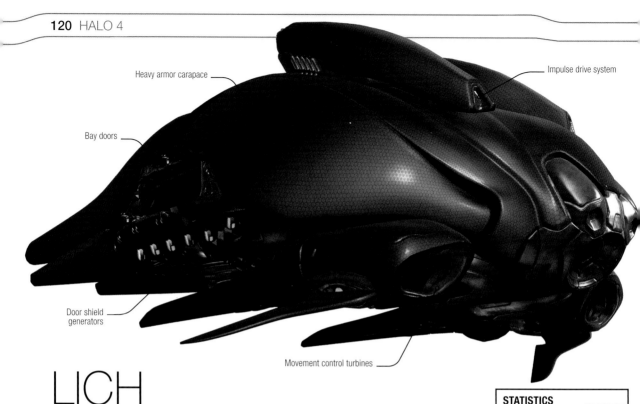

Heavy armor carapace

Impulse drive system

Bay doors

Door shield
generators

Movement control turbines

LICH

DEPLOYMENT PLATFORM
T-56 GROUND SUPPORT/ULTRA HEAVY

Outside of space, Covenant mass deployment platforms were rarely encountered during the Human-Covenant War. Designed by Achoem Weapons of the Sanghelios' continent of Tolvuus, the T-56 Lich is an example of relatively unknown platform that only came to the forefront during the conflict on Requiem. This well-armored, multi-cabin vessel was created to quickly and safely deploy extremely large numbers of troops into an area that conventional deployment methods could not sufficiently handle. Although most Lich vehicles are well-guarded by a number of squads and turrets, its lack of any significant on-ship defenses make it somewhat vulnerable to infiltration.

STATISTICS

MANUFACTURER
Achoem Weapons

CREW CAPACITY
30–40 personnel

PRIMARY ARMAMENT
T-56 PEW/M

SECONDARY ARMAMEMNT
T-52 DESW (4)

LENGTH
337.2ft (102.8m)

WIDTH
166.9ft (50.9m)

HEIGHT
113.9ft (34.7m)

The T-56 Lich's multi-tiered bay door offers its crew an elevated perch to survey the battlefield.

The T-53 Squad Breaching Carapace has been observed in combat deploying a small number of Covenant troops.

Mounting arms

COVENANT DROP POD

T-51 INDIVIDUAL BREACHING CARAPACE

Likely the most varied of all Covenant transportation methods, humanity has only scratched the surface of the differing formats these drop pods have displayed over the course of the war. The most prominent drop pod currently used by the Covenant is the T-51 IBC (Individual Breaching Carapace). Although larger than the individual pods launched in the past, these pods are smaller than full deployment carapaces that convey numerous enemies. The purpose of breaching vessels such as these is to infiltrate planetary or ship-based defenses with both discretion and speed.

STATISTICS

MANUFACTURER
Lodam Armory

CREW CAPACITY
1–5 personnel

LENGTH
12.8ft (3.9m)

WIDTH
12.9ft (3.9m)

HEIGHT
26.4ft (8m)

Forward-braking system

Terrain-locking prongs

COVENANT ORBITAL POD

T-54 MASS DEPLOYMENT CARAPACE

Distinct from smaller drop pods and other multi-troop deployment systems, the T-54 MDC (Mass Deployment Carapace) isn't as much a distribution method as it is a transportation apparatus. Lodged into large-scale capital ships, the deployment carapace is expelled toward a planet's surface or into the heart of an enemy vessel, its infantry are released, and then it quickly launches back toward its point of origin, recoupling with the capital ship and embarking more passengers for another deployment. Although originally implemented to avoid costs incurred when drop pods were abandoned, this has become an exceptionally practical method of troop distribution.

Deployed troops are locked into one of several tiers as the pod descends and just before being released into combat.

STATISTICS

MANUFACTURER
Lodam Armory

CREW CAPACITY
15–20 personnel

LENGTH
73.4ft (22.4m)

WIDTH
82.1ft (25m)

HEIGHT
106ft (32.3m)

Mounting arms

Impulse drive systems

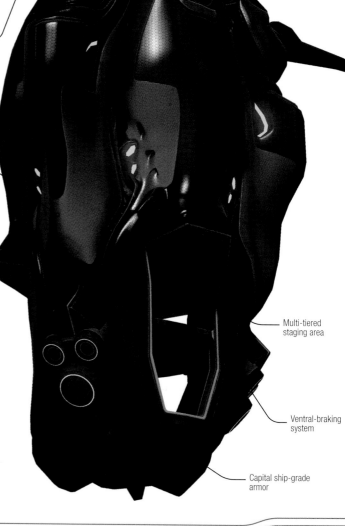

Multi-tiered staging area

Ventral-braking system

Capital ship-grade armor

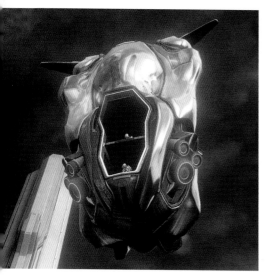

Using a low-range gravity dampening pulse, infantry are able to safely drop from the pod bay to the ground.

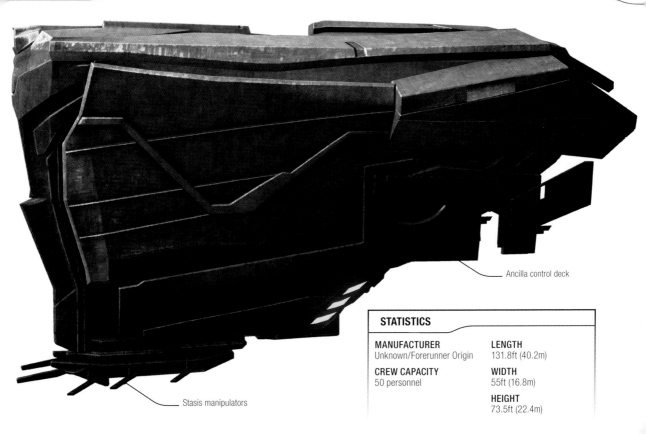

Ancilla control deck

Stasis manipulators

STATISTICS	
MANUFACTURER Unknown/Forerunner Origin	**LENGTH** 131.8ft (40.2m)
CREW CAPACITY 50 personnel	**WIDTH** 55ft (16.8m)
	HEIGHT 73.5ft (22.4m)

FORERUNNER ESCORT

Z-330 INDEPENDENT ACTUATION DEFENSE ESCORT/HEAVY

Within the Didact's massive warship, *Mantle's Approach*, reports indicate that he utilized a number of sizable escort vessels (which were either controlled by individual ancilla constructs or through some automated means) to defend this ship during the assault on New Phoenix. The full functionality and purpose of these escorts are unknown, but it appears that these vessels were previously used to ferry individuals and equipment through the vast interior of the Forerunner ship, with limited mobility outside of this capacity. Escort vessels such as these were oftentimes circumvented by leaner, fully weaponized and armored combat suits such as war sphinxes.

Escorts were stationed near the Didact during his attack of Earth.

CRYOTUBE

MARK-VIII CRYOGENIC SUSPENSION CHAMBER

Cryostorage apparatuses such as cryotubes (or "chambers") are stasis compartments within human space-faring vessels that allow organic bodies to endure protracted journeys for several months at a time. A chemical called cytoprethaline is injected into subjects before they are sealed into the chamber, preventing the crystallization of cells before entering a deep sleep. Not only do subjects age at a significantly slower rate while in cryo, but their bodies are carefully preserved, allowing healthy and safe transportation across space. Although cryostorage has become a standard part of 26th-century life, it is not without risk: Due to chemical allergies, some subjects endure debilitating health after awaking from sleep.

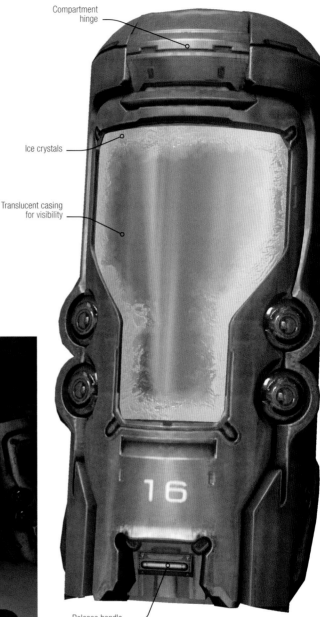

Compartment hinge

Ice crystals

Translucent casing for visibility

16

Release handle

In cryostasis, a subject's physical growth is almost completely stunted, and in cases of extreme length, this can create a discontinuity margin between the subject's chronological age and their biological age.

STATISTICS

MANUFACTURER Jakubaitis Standard Systems	**WIDTH** 5.1ft (1.6m)
USAGE Cryostorage	**HEIGHT** 11.3ft (3.4m)
LENGTH 7.4ft (2.3m)	

STATISTICS

MANUFACTURER
Misriah Armory

USAGE
Ordnance Deployment

LENGTH
32.9in (83.5cm)

WIDTH
32.5in (82.5cm)

HEIGHT
95.3in (242.1cm)

Upon impact, gas-pressured releases splay the pod open in order to reveal its provided ordnance.

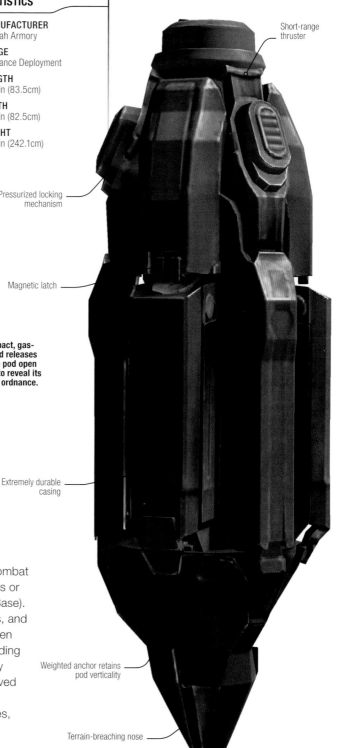

Short-range thruster

Pressurized locking mechanism

Magnetic latch

Extremely durable casing

Weighted anchor retains pod verticality

Terrain-breaching nose

ORDNANCE POD

M2859 MATERIEL ACQUISITION POD

Now commonplace within the UNSC, Materiel Acquisition Pods (MAP), generally referred to as "ordnance pods," are often fired into challenging combat theaters, particularly those deep behind enemy lines or well outside range of an FOB (Forward Operating Base). Ordnance pods are fitted with weapons, explosives, and other military hardware, launched from the air or even suborbital positions, impaling the ground and providing nearby infantry with viable equipment. Although any weapon can be affixed to a pod, most pods are saved for heavy materiel, munitions, and explosives, or long-range equipment. During War Games exercises, Spartan-IV personnel are trained to effectively call in ordnance pods in any circumstance.

Markers maintain extremely high usage restrictions.

After keying in a destination, the beacon becomes active, lighting up while preparing to send the marked packages.

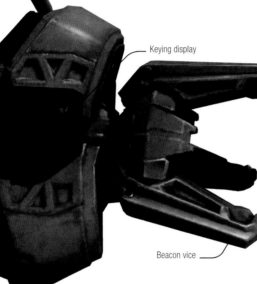

Stabilizing grip

Keying display

Beacon vice

Plane emitter housing

Translocation beacon

QUANTUM MARKER

MX-1050 QUANTUM PLANE TRANSLOCATION MARKER - LOCAL/HYBRID

The MX-1050 Quantum Marker is a prototype handheld device borne out of ONI's translocation grid testing conducted on a variety of Forerunner installations. Currently in the testing phase, it is ultimately intended to be used for the immediate transportation of assets from hostile environments. After enclosing an asset in a slipspace-shielded containment unit, operators dispatch a translocation beacon using the marker. Within a matter of seconds, the beacon jettisons the containment unit offsite to a precalibrated receiver node, generally a great distance away. Although native translocation technology allows the transportation of organic matter, operators are expressly forbidden to use the MX-1050 in this manner, as it is unproven and considered extremely dangerous.

STATISTICS

MANUFACTURER
Acheron Security

USAGE
Translocation Marking

LENGTH—Marker
25.5in (64.7cm)

WIDTH—Marker
16.3in (41.5cm)

HEIGHT—Marker
17.7in (45cm)

LENGTH—Beacon
6.9in (17.6cm)

WIDTH—Beacon
6.8in (17.3cm)

HEIGHT—Beacon
6.6in (16.8cm)

TERMINAL

Z-9930 INFORMATION VECTOR CONSOLE

Littered across most Forerunner constructs are
terminals, which can be accessed via properly
acclimated AIs or native ancillas. In general,
terminals are databases of knowledge and past
experiences, but many operate simply as
a conduit for information transmitted from
a source called the Domain. This is believed
to be a transcendent quantum repository of
Forerunner history that suffered major lapses
toward the end of their civilization's existence.
On Installation 00, the Master Chief communicated
with the malfunctioning but penitent Mendicant
Bias through terminals, and while on Requiem,
Cortana managed to retrieve ancient secrets that
had been buried by Forerunners just before their
galaxy-wide extinction.

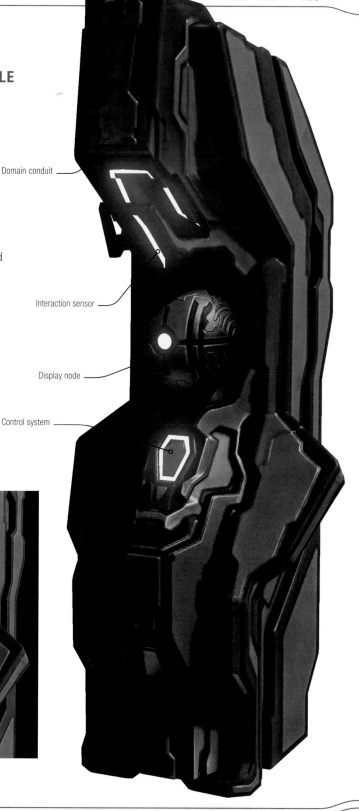

Domain conduit

Interaction sensor

Display node

Control system

STATISTICS

MANUFACTURER Unknown/Forerunner Origin	**WIDTH** 4.5ft (1.4m)
USAGE Network Console	**HEIGHT** 10.6ft (3.2m)
LENGTH 4.9ft (1.5m)	

**This terminal was hidden within the excavated
rubble of Installation 03.**

HARVESTER

T-58 ULTRA-HEAVY SITE EXCAVATOR/EMBEDDED

Recently discovered on the Forerunner shield world of Requiem, detachments of the newly formed Covenant under Jul 'Mdama have been witnessed operating an impressive tier-five excavator machine that is similar in function to the T-30 Locust and the T-36 and T-47 Scarab, though dramatically different in shape, size, and mobility.

Referred to simply as Harvesters, these large, arachnid-like vehicles are organic in design, showing a clear Hesduros heritage, though they appear to be yet another variation of the Lekgolo (possibly Sbaolekgolo), where a meta-colony is established within a vehicle to move and drive it, under the guidance of an operator.

STATISTICS

MANUFACTURER
Lodam Armory

USAGE
Deep Excavation

LENGTH
719.4–892.4ft (219.2–272m)

WIDTH
485.2–911.3ft (147.9–277.8m)

HEIGHT
438.8–546.2ft (133.8–166.5m)

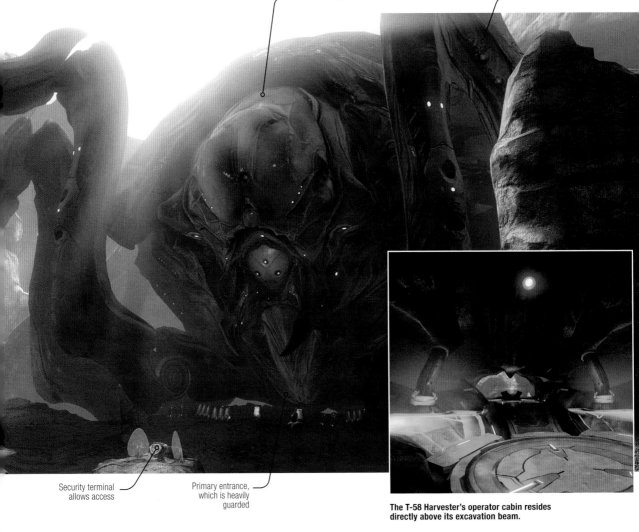

Heavily armored hull

Legs are used for stability and movement

Security terminal allows access

Primary entrance, which is heavily guarded

The T-58 Harvester's operator cabin resides directly above its excavation beam.

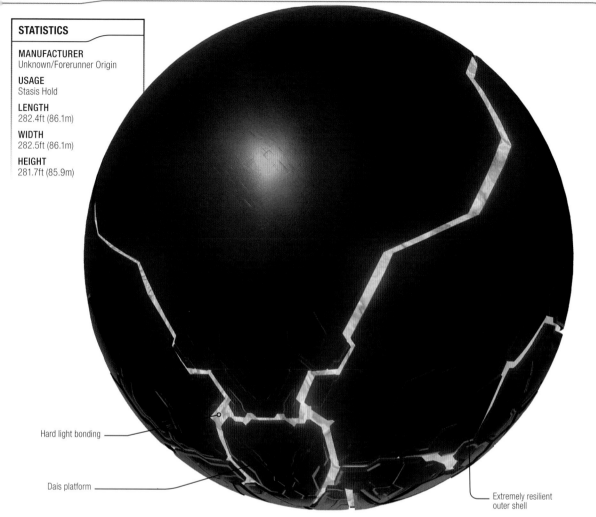

STATISTICS

MANUFACTURER
Unknown/Forerunner Origin

USAGE
Stasis Hold

LENGTH
282.4ft (86.1m)

WIDTH
282.5ft (86.1m)

HEIGHT
281.7ft (85.9m)

Hard light bonding

Dais platform

Extremely resilient
outer shell

CRYPTUM

WARRIOR KEEP

Often referred to as a "Warrior Keep," a Cryptum is a Forerunner apparatus that can hypothetically maintain and protect a physical being over long periods of time, while they are in a deep state of meditation referred to as "xankara." This state can be maintained for many millennia, effectively locking away the being in an immobile and inert state. During their time in the galaxy, Forerunners used this form of exile for most of their rates, when other punishments were deemed too severe. The most notable usage was with Prometheans (hence the name "Warrior Keep"), and, in particular, the renowned and formidable Didact.

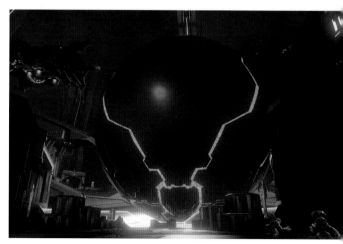

The Didact's own combat Cryptum was retrieved from his ship and used to lock him away in the heart of Requiem.

ONI excavated the Composer and brought it to Ivanoff Station.

Targeting mechanism

Sublimation relay

COMPOSER

FORERUNNER SUBLIMATION DEVICE

The Composer is a Forerunner device used to transform (or compose) a sentient being into a collection of data, sometimes referred to as an "essence." Although the process is extremely painful and irreversible, the data could be transferred into a number of different machines or durances for safekeeping. The initial hope was that the Composer could eventually grant immortality, allowing Forerunners to integrate old essences into youthful bodies. Unfortunately, efforts to this end only led to tragic aberrations and death. In an act of horror, the Didact would use the Composer to transform ancient humans into his own warrior slaves—the mechanized creatures now known as Prometheans.

STATISTICS

MANUFACTURER
Unknown/Forerunner Origin

USAGE
Sublimation Device

LENGTH
126.7ft (38.6m)

WIDTH
94.2ft (28.7m)

HEIGHT
681ft (207.6m)

SENTINEL

Z-1500 AUTOMATED SYSTEMS DRONE

Based on all anecdotal data, Sentinels appear to have been the main functionary drone of most Forerunner sites, providing automated support for many thousands of years at a time. Sentinels come in a variety of sizes and shapes, ranging from the small and delicate Constructors, which flit about, building out and repairing the fabric of a site's constitution to Retrievers—massive ship-like machines with enormous manipulators and excavation systems, allowing them to mine for important resources from a given site. The most common Sentinel is easily the Aggressor—an automated yet versatile defensive drone that has been used to swiftly target and destroy any perceived threat.

Manipulators

Central processor housing

Boom arm

STATISTICS

MANUFACTURER
Unknown/Forerunner Origin

USAGE
Defense Drone

LENGTH
9.6ft (2.9m)

WIDTH
6.3ft (1.9m)

HEIGHT
5ft (1.5m)

Energy beam emitter

These drones use an exotic type of impulse drive to fly, but can also tap into their installation's translocation grid.

External container

Durance shell

Percussive
breaching system

Imprint matrix
locked within

DURANCE

IMPRINT MATRIX

Acquired by a Spartan fireteam from the Requiem site known as "the Cauldron," the artifact referred to by the Covenant as "the Didact's Gift" was actually a modified Forerunner durance, used by the Didact to contain and transfer essences culled from victims of the Composer. Historically, durances had been used to store Forerunner imprints, memorializing their immolated remains and patterns

deep into the future, as the Didact was forced to do with his children during the course of the war with ancient humans. With the Composer, the Didact was able to uses durances like this one to continue populating his army of Prometheans with enslaved human essences.

**Fireteam Majestic
secured a durance
on Requiem.**

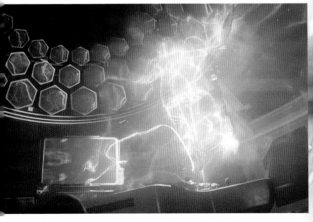

During *Infinity*'s campaign on Requiem, the contents of a durance were suddenly exposed, revealing the tragic result of the Didact's assault of New Phoenix.

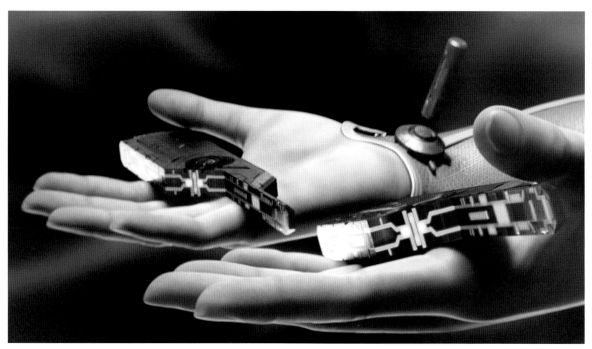

JANUS KEY

FORERUNNER CARTOGRAPHER

Long since hidden on the shield world of Requiem, the Janus Key is a Forerunner artifact of extraordinary importance, which has remained concealed until it was discovered by Spartan teams deployed to counter Covenant excavation sites. According to the Librarian, this artifact was intended to provide real-time locational data to all Forerunner technologies, giving the holder incredible power upon bringing the key to a location referred to as the Absolute Record. The Librarian had hoped the Didact's time in the Cryptum would have righted his understanding of the Mantle, allowing him to assist humanity on the path toward bearing it. Unfortunately, this result was not achieved and now the Janus Key is split between the Covenant and the UNSC, as the power it holds hangs in the balance.

STATISTICS

MANUFACTURER
Unknown/Forerunner Origin

USAGE
Galactic Cartographer

LENGTH—Complete key
5.6in (14.2cm)

WIDTH—Complete key
1.2in (3cm)

HEIGHT—Complete key
1.9in (4.9cm)

LENGTH—Single key
5.5in (14cm)

WIDTH—Single key
1.2in (3cm)

HEIGHT—Single key
1.4in (3.5cm)

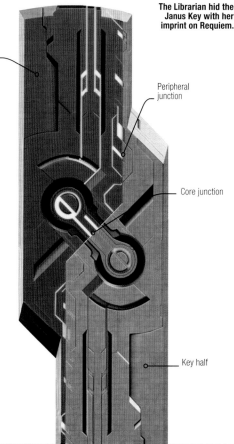

The Librarian hid the Janus Key with her imprint on Requiem.

Key half

Peripheral junction

Core junction

Key half

Despite the slight shimmer of refracted light, this module generally provides effective camouflage.

As Majestic discovered on Requiem, Active Camouflage apparatuses can vary in size and shape.

ACTIVE CAMOUFLAGE

T-3 REFRACTION DISSONANCE MODIFIER/CAMOUFLAGE

Active Camouflage, a refraction dissonance modifier that can bend light around the surface of an individual or structure, was deemed a key alien technology early on, extensively researched by ONI during the first few years of the war. Over the course of the conflict, it was wielded impressively by many Sangheili—usually those found in Special Operations or Zealot classes. However, ONI's breakthroughs here have led to ad hoc compatibility with certain armor and BDU types, the most prominent and notable being that of Mjolnir, as worn by Spartans. With this equipped, a soldier can effectively pass through an area unnoticed, bearing only a slight refractive shimmer while mobile.

STATISTICS	
MANUFACTURER	Merchants of Qikost
USAGE	Armor Optimization
LENGTH	2.5in (6.3cm)
WIDTH	12.1in (30.6cm)
HEIGHT	4.4in (11.3cm)

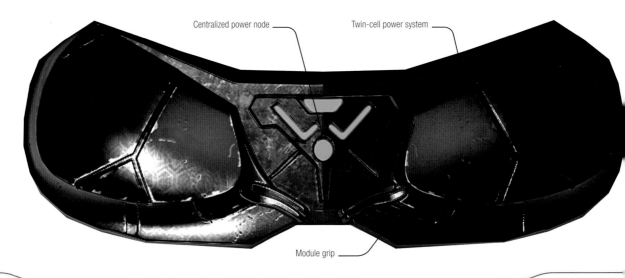

Centralized power node

Twin-cell power system

Module grip

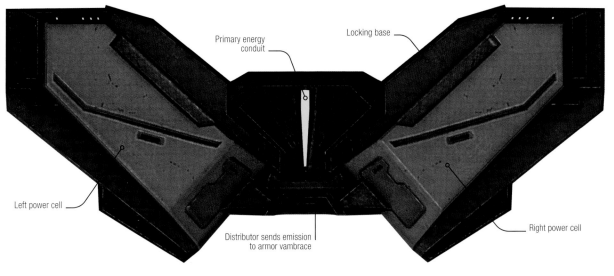

Primary energy conduit

Locking base

Left power cell

Distributor sends emission to armor vambrace

Right power cell

HARDLIGHT SHIELD

Z-90 PHOTONIC COALESCENCE EMITTER/AEGIS

As incorporated by many other Forerunner technological applications, the Hardlight Shield is composed of a photon emitter that can actively fuse its particles of light into a rigid, though dissipative, barrier. The composition of hard light can bear varying degrees of solidity, but within the context of the Hardlight Shield, it is only considered ruggedly resistive, not impervious. This is likely due to the module's inability to propagate wide-range power generation. Although ONI has utilized a number of portable energy shields from previous Covenant technology, the best application of hard light has come directly from the Forerunners, and more specifically the Prometheans of Requiem.

STATISTICS
MANUFACTURER Unknown/Forerunner Origin
USAGE Armor Optimization
LENGTH—Apparatus 1.5in (3.9cm)
WIDTH—Apparatus 13.5in (34.3cm)
HEIGHT—Apparatus 5.6in (14.3cm)
LENGTH—Shield 29.7in (75.5cm)
WIDTH—Shield 79.3in (201.3cm)
HEIGHT—Shield 103.6in (263.2cm)

Conduits draw excess energy from the armor to form the shield at its vambrace.

All contemporary Mjolnir systems utilize personal energy shields, but the Hardlight Shield effectively provides additional defense when needed.

The VISR technology separates friend from foe for its user.

PROMETHEAN VISION

Z-5080 SHORT-RANGE SPECTRUM AUGMENTER/VISION

For centuries, humans have used a wide range of visual enhancement technologies, many of which have been applied to VISR (Visual Intelligence System, Reconnaissance) combat applications. When Prometheans on Requiem were discovered using short-range, full-spectrum enhancement modules, these were woven into the existing Mjolnir GEN2 composition as a variant of the stabilized VISR 4.0 technology suite. Many contemporary Spartans utilize some form of Promethean Vision as a Mjolnir-mounted armor ability, allowing them to see allies, enemies, and some ordnance through solid surfaces. This tactical advantage has been the source of many victories for the UNSC while deployed on Requiem.

Primary energy conduit

Distributor sends spectrum augmentation to VISR 4.0 suite

STATISTICS	
MANUFACTURER	Unknown/Forerunner Origin
USAGE	Armor Optimization
LENGTH	1.5in (3.9cm)
WIDTH	13.5in (34.3cm)
HEIGHT	5.6in (14.3cm)

HOLOGRAM

T-27 RESPONSIVE HOLOGRAPHIC FORM EMULATOR

The decoy package known as "Hologram" is the result of technology captured from Kig-Yar feint devices, as encountered with Skirmisher squads on the colonies of Hat Yai, Actium, and Reach, among others. After numerous tests, ONI managed to successfully reverse engineer the technology and incorporate it into Mjolnir's GEN1 and GEN2 firmware. In its current state, holographic decoy is essentially a response emulator that fabricates an incredibly realistic holographic copy of the user's physical body and movement. When properly applied, the ONI-engineered variant allows Spartans to create a decoy as a ruse during combat, tricking enemies into revealing their position and vulnerabilities.

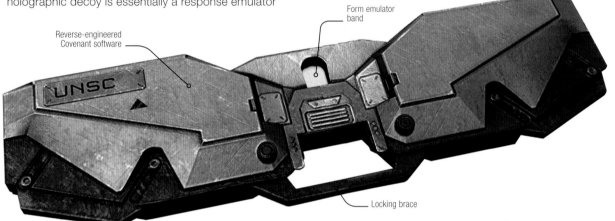

Form emulator band

Reverse-engineered Covenant software

Locking brace

STATISTICS

MANUFACTURER
Materials Group

USAGE
Armor Optimization

LENGTH
1.8in (4.5cm)

WIDTH
13.2in (33.5cm)

HEIGHT
4in (10.2cm)

Decoys are incredibly lifelike and often feint enemies into revealing their own positions.

AUTOSENTRY

Z-2500 AUTOMATED PROTECTION DRONE

First encountered defending a number of Requiem's Promethean classes, the Autosentry was initially believed to be an autonomous, self-sustained defensive drone that is native to the shield world, and similar to the Sentinel. Only later was it discovered that the drone was actually created ad hoc by the Prometheans themselves, materialized through hard light as a combat support drone. The UNSC employs a number of automated protection drones of varying intelligence and quality, but the integration of Forerunner socket modules from Promethean armor has allowed Mjolnir GEN2-armored Spartans to leverage these specific Autosentry units in combat.

STATISTICS

MANUFACTURER Unknown/Forerunner Origin	**HEIGHT—Apparatus** 5.6in (14.3cm)
USAGE Armor Optimization	**LENGTH—Sentry** 56.7in (144cm)
LENGTH—Apparatus 1.5in (3.9cm)	**WIDTH—Sentry** 39.1in (99.3cm)
WIDTH—Apparatus 13.5in (34.3cm)	**HEIGHT—Sentry** 30.4in (77.2cm)

Pivoting hover movement

Firing lens

Targeting array

The Autosentry can be spontaneously deployed by a Spartan to provide suppressive fire and new tactical opportunities.

Jet Packs offer practical combat solutions, such as providing an elevated position.

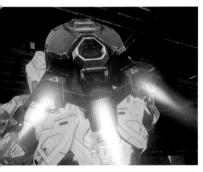

S-12 systems maintain three separate thrusters.

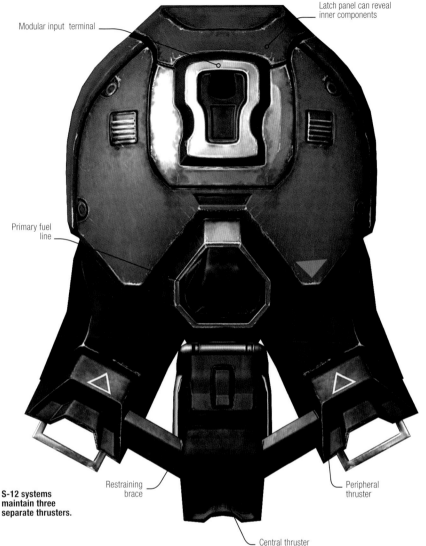

Modular input terminal

Latch panel can reveal inner components

Primary fuel line

Restraining brace

Peripheral thruster

Central thruster

JET PACK

SERIES 12 SINGLE OPERATOR LIFT APPARATUS

Nearly all space-active combat elements within the UNSC are extensively trained with jump-jet packs, which are essentially single operator lift apparatuses used for gravity mitigation, re-entry stabilization, and all manner of EVA mobility. Lethbridge Industrial has, in many respects, led this field, working with all BDU and armor programs to create appropriate jet pack solutions that can be used by anyone from service-specific personnel and grunt infantry to ODSTs, Spartans, and even Delta-Six operators. Most S-IV personnel utilize Series 12 SOLA units to navigate the corridors of massive starship interiors, or to effect combat around large bases and vehicles.

STATISTICS	
MANUFACTURER	Lethbridge Industrial
USAGE	Armor Optimization
LENGTH	9.6in (24.3cm)
WIDTH	16.2in (41.2cm)
HEIGHT	21in (53.1cm)

Regen fields are often used to strategically augment allies when assaulting an enemy territory.

A Spartan is more resilient when fighting from within a Regen Field.

REGENERATION FIELD

M2705 REGENERATIVE KINETIC DISPERSAL FIELD

Although its driving mechanisms are generally disputed outside of Acheron Security, the armor ability known as Regeneration Field has been widely adopted by Spartan-IVs in combat. This coupling socket allows users to generate a quick burst of shunting energy, forcing FOF-designated enemies away momentarily while simultaneously generating a component-stabilizing field which can recharge the combat viability of nearby allies, including their armor shielding. It is believed that this is accomplished through a number of short-term power reappropriations, but the origin of this specific technology is heavily classified, per ONI-authored contractor obligation clauses.

STATISTICS

MANUFACTURER
Acheron Security

USAGE
Armor Optimization

LENGTH—Apparatus
1.8in (4.5cm)

WIDTH—Apparatus
13.2in (33.5cm)

HEIGHT—Apparatus
4in (10.2cm)

THRUSTER PACK

M805X FORWARD ACCELERATION SYSTEM - FULCRUM MITIGATING

Yet another EVA-focused armor component manufactured by Lethbridge Industrial, the Thruster Pack is intended to be a forward acceleration system that can launch personnel across a horizontal plane without the need for a pivot point or leveraging fulcrum. Unlike jump-jet packs, which are a far broader field of gravity mitigation apparatuses (both combative and non-combative), Thruster Packs are intended to provide users real time advantages within battle, jettisoning them in a specific direction to evade or assault enemies. Although this is referred to as a "forward" acceleration due to its most common usage, operators are capable of movement in any direction across a horizontal plane.

Central thruster stack

Transverse binding plate

Right thruster stack

Left thruster stack

STATISTICS	
MANUFACTURER	Lethbridge Industrial
USAGE	Armor Optimization
LENGTH	4in (10.2cm)
WIDTH	19.2in (48.7cm)
HEIGHT	14.6in (37.2cm)

Properly trained Spartans can effectively leverage the Thruster Pack to a great degree in combat.

ARMOR

AIR ASSAULT

MJOLNIR POWERED ASSAULT ARMOR [GEN2] - AIR ASSAULT

All Mjolnir armor systems that were designed for airborne combat actuation were originally spearheaded and refined by the Ushuaia Armory based out of Reach. Initially, these armor systems were created for Army airborne personnel and S-II/S-III operators who were deployed to suborbital facilities with harsh environments, such as skyhooks and tethers in a planet's stratosphere. With the destruction of Reach, the privately owned Naphtali Contractor Corporation on Earth acquired the original designs and prepared a GEN2 variant for Spartan-IVs, which now provides functional support across a number of colonies as well as remotely deployed combat units.

AIR ASSAULT-class armor was tested in the Cascadian city of Mindoro.

Integrated comm network

Locking retrieval brace

Low-drag pauldron system

AIR ASSAULT meets all the Ordnance Commission strictures for groundside combat.

STATISTICS

MANUFACTURER
Naphtali Contractor Corporation

LOCATION
Abilene, North America, EARTH

TESTING SITE
Buffalo Breaker Yards

With the increased production of both Sabre and Broadsword fighters, AVIATOR-class armor has become more popular among Spartans.

STATISTICS

MANUFACTURER
Hannibal Weapon Systems

LOCATION
Kotka, Pori, NEW CARTHAGE

TESTING SITE
WG/Facility 93-00/Kotka

Pilot-centric
HUD integration

Pressure-stabilized
rebreather feed

Rigid collar to
mitigate flight duress

AVIATOR

MJOLNIR POWERED ASSAULT ARMOR [GEN2] - AVIATOR

One of the most intriguing armor systems to arise from the post-war Mjolnir collaboration is easily GEN2's AVIATOR-class. For decades, the notion of specialized pilot armor for Spartans seemed redundant, given existing Mjolnir variants were already suitable for such rigors. With the segregation of Spartan-IVs into their own autonomous branch, however, the need for multiple intra-organizational disciplines materialized. Built from the ground up by Hannibal Weapon Systems for Spartan pilots, AVIATOR-class armor is designed for the operation of Longswords, Sabres, Broadswords, and even Shortsword suborbital bombers.

CIO's central focus is on espionage, not lethality.

C.I.O.

MJOLNIR POWERED ASSAULT ARMOR [GEN2] - COUNTER-INTELLIGENCE OPERABILITY

Extremely rare, even within remote deployment units, these armor systems were designed for counter-intelligence operability and generally serve one strategic purpose: the acquisition of intel behind enemy lines. Seeing the need for highly trained, heavily armored personnel to be deployed deep in enemy-controlled territory, Acheron Security developed CIO-class armor, worn by Spartans who endure tier-nine theaters in order to acquire critical, strategic data from opposing forces. Although highly classified, the most notable deployment of CIO-armored Spartans was likely Terceira, where several operatives captured and transmitted info that was crucial to the recovery of the colony from rebel forces.

Tricloptically fixed multi-spectral imaging array

Modular sensory suite

Silhouette dampener for motion sensor circumvention

Due to its exclusivity, only a handful of active operatives currently use CIO.

STATISTICS

MANUFACTURER
Acheron Security

LOCATION
Gdynia, Acheron Fossae, MARS

TESTING SITE
Acheron Trauma Sim

STATISTICS

MANUFACTURER
Naphtali Contractor Corporation

LOCATION
Abilene, North America, EARTH

TESTING SITE
Buffalo Breaker Yards

Possibly a vestige of tradition, many team leaders still select COMMANDO systems.

COMMANDO

Field elaboration software for real-time combat intel modification

Onboard CNM suite for tactical application

MJOLNIR POWERED ASSAULT ARMOR [GEN2] - COMMANDO

After the planet Meridian was attacked by the Covenant, all of the contracts previously afforded to the local Chalybs Defense Solutions firm were absorbed by private materiel manufacturers who had survived the war. COMMANDO-class armor found its way into the hands of the Naphtali Contractor Corporation, who would circumvent the existing limitations of the GEN1 system, prying it away from a semi-exclusive hardware for team leaders and tactical command operatives. The GEN2 variant has expanded across all roles, maintaining an elaborate CNM (Command Network Module) suite, uplink functionality, and logistical software.

Fireteam allocation module (wide-range)

This armor was originally conceived for Special Forces operatives, earning it the name COMMANDO.

DEFENDER

MJOLNIR POWERED ASSAULT ARMOR [GEN2] - DEFENDER

Shortly after the end of the war, the Ordnance Commission validated the need for specialized, defense-centric armor variants, which were used for the protection of civilian populations rather than the assault of enemy strongholds. On Luna, the Imbrium Machine Complex developed DEFENDER-class armor, which, despite following the various strictures of the Commission's rulings, still managed to be an incredibly effective combat system. DEFENDER-class armor is generally used on controller bases, a handful of classified ONI sites, and in some colonial populations where civil unrest is common.

STATISTICS

MANUFACTURER
Imbrium Machine Complex

LOCATION
Ankara, Mare Imbrium, LUNA

TESTING SITE
Anakara Resiliency Chamber

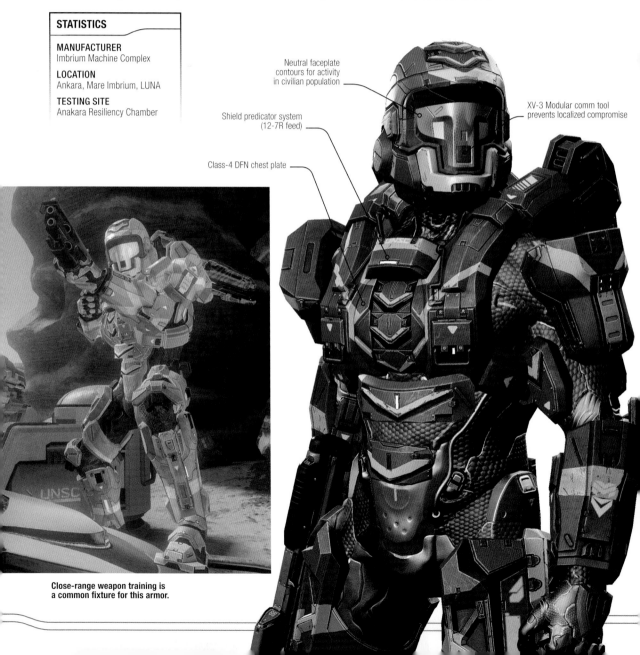

Neutral faceplate contours for activity in civilian population

Shield predicator system (12-7R feed)

Class-4 DFN chest plate

XV-3 Modular comm tool prevents localized compromise

Close-range weapon training is a common fixture for this armor.

EOD has seen a handful of variants since its inception at the end of the Covenant War.

STATISTICS

MANUFACTURER
Naphtali Contractor Corporation

LOCATION
Abilene, North America, EARTH

TESTING SITE
Buffalo Breaker Yards

Alternating heat balance drives

Pressure-resistant hardened rebreather unit

Flow-distributing ceramic plates

E.O.D.

MJOLNIR POWERED ASSAULT ARMOR [GEN2] - EXPLOSIVE ORDNANCE DISPOSAL

Designed for explosive ordnance disposal, the origin of EOD-class armor is something of a legend among Spartans. When the original S-II class was deployed to Chi Ceti IV in an effort to acquire the first line of Mjolnir armor, one of their own was sacrificed in a tragic explosion while defending the facility from the Covenant. In response, the Materials Group devised a number of solutions in an attempt to thwart future disasters of the same nature. In 2554, they would transfer the manufacturing contract to the Naphtali Contractor Corporation, who had proposed additional enhancements to the armor's systemic approach to the GEN2 framework, which would be used primarily by Spartan-IVs.

STATISTICS

MANUFACTURER
Imbrium Machine Complex

LOCATION
Ankara, Mare Imbrium, LUNA

TESTING SITE
Anakara Resiliency Chamber

Cycloptic field assessing module for tactical awareness

Open-line channel modifier for power conservation

Security executor roles have become more common in the aftermath of the Covenant War.

Twin L-4 component feeds

ENFORCER

MJOLNIR POWERED ASSAULT ARMOR [GEN2] - ENFORCER

ENFORCER-class armor was designed in the foothills of Ankara by Imbrium Machine Complex. It is a security executor system utilized by Spartans who operate on remote bases with a native battle network or a co-opted enemy network. The armor is designed to provide specific benefits for personnel engaged in defensive maneuvers, those simply operating from a localized site, or those deployed to enemy-held locations for policing purposes. The most recent iteration of the armor passed tests per Ankara Field Stricture BL58-0, leading to its approval by the Damascus Ordnance Commission, and eventually becoming an ONI prerequisite for service at a handful of very specific ZULU-level facilities.

E.V.A.

MJOLNIR POWERED ASSAULT ARMOR [GEN2] - EXTRA VEHICULAR ACTIVITY

The most commonly utilized Mjolnir armor variant outside baseline systems, EVA-class armor was conceived for extra-vehicular activity, despite the fact that standard Mjolnir systems are already compliant with vacuum operational requirements. What EVA provides that other armor systems do not is an aggressive optimization on survivability in infantry-based space combat, or combat that occurs in hostile exoatmospheric environments with extremely low-gravity to zero-gravity. The Materials Group, which spearheaded the GEN1 variant, has continued to manufacture this system's GEN2 cycle, although other companies have attempted to closely emulate the work already done here in order to establish alternate EVA-focused systems.

EVA has seen the least physical variation since its inception.

STATISTICS

MANUFACTURER
Materials Group

LOCATION
Swanbourne, Australia, EARTH

TESTING SITE
WG/Facility 58-32/B5D

Open-view visor system typical of EVA configurations

Larger pauldron silhouette than previous models

59-L20 Aureole braces for awareness improvement

Slim-contoured chest plate lowers physical profile dramatically

Materials Group retains EVA production rights due to their long-standing history of investment.

GUNGNIR

MJOLNIR POWERED ASSAULT ARMOR [GEN2] - GUNGNIR

GUNGNIR-class armor was originally conceived of as an optical targeting companion to the M6 Nonlinear Rifle—a weapon colloquially referred to as the Spartan Laser. During early GEN1 prototypes, Spartans fielded this armor and weapon against the Covenant, leveraging its Wyrd III sensory optimization for long-range, high-impact materiel strikes.

Despite its exclusivity, even well before the GEN1 line expired, many Spartans had already adopted this armor regardless of weapon loadout, preferring its isolated video optics and enhanced cranial plating for combat in unshielded locations or with exposure to intense flare radiometric conditions, as experienced at a variety of Covenant manufacturing sites.

Enhanced cranial plating

Wyrd III integrated video optics

Centralized power-distribution capacitor (Servo L-903)

Breach-anchored collar system for in-field modification

Early prototypes of this armor were first tested against the Covenant.

Most high-powered weapons pair well with GUNGNIR, despite its early exclusivity to nonlinear rifles.

MANUFACTURER
Acheron Security

LOCATION
Gdynia, Acheron Fossae, MARS

TESTING SITE
Acheron Trauma Sim

HAZOP is generally deployed to exotic locales.

Modified rebreather caster lines

Firm-case fusion pack to simplify withdrawal process

View-path stabilizing visor with AZ-T sensor array

Redundant oxygen filtration system (Unit A-7X43)

HAZOP

MJOLNIR POWERED ASSAULT ARMOR [GEN2] - HAZARDOUS OPERABILITY

Hazardous Operability armor was spearheaded by the Materials Group out of Damascus in order to further augment the Mjolnir line in situations where personnel were engaged in hazardous locales and endured excessive contact with radiation, volatiles, toxins, or other problematic elements. Templates for the GEN2 variant of HAZOP-class armor were acquired by Acheron Security in 2553, where a number of advances were engineered to enhance protective operability during EVA deployment outside a vessel while it was in slipspace. Progress in this capacity remains slow and tentative, but many Spartans have already adopted the GEN2 framework for HAZOP.

Almost exclusively designed for irruption maneuvers, some Spartans prefer INFILTRATOR's less opaque stealth features over other armor systems.

STATISTICS

MANUFACTURER
Hannibal Weapon Systems

LOCATION
Kotka, Pori, NEW CARTHAGE

TESTING SITE
WG/Facility 93-00/Kotka

Wide-range approach tracking feed

Hardened-uplink node for off-world communication

Q9L-3 Kotka comm-veil for transmission masking

Ingress cloaking module to mask motion silhouette at most spectrums

INFILTRATOR

MJOLNIR POWERED ASSAULT ARMOR [GEN2] - INFILTRATOR

INFILTRATOR-class armor is relatively new to the Mjolnir platform. It is intended for stealth operations, giving Spartans the ability to subvert and penetrate defensive and security systems of extremely fortified sites. Created by Hannibal Weapon Systems out of New Carthage, INFILTRATOR-class armor was tested under extraordinary conditions. Jettisoned from high above the planet, Spartans testing the armor were forced to use re-entry packs to reach heavily protected weapon platforms, infiltrating them to accomplish specific objectives and escape without being hindered by passive inhibitors or guards. These tests proved successful in honing one of Mjolnir's best GEN2 armor variants.

MARK VI

MJOLNIR POWERED ASSAULT ARMOR [GEN1] - MARK VI

Revered due to its renowned legacy, Mjolnir's standard Mark VI armor set is still considered GEN1 despite having adopted numerous GEN2 improvements and even being used by contemporary Spartan-IVs in combat. This armor gained notice when it was used by the Master Chief to defend Earth and bring the war to an end on the Forerunner installation known as the Ark. Reports indicate that a number of remaining Spartan-IIs still use standard Mark VI and its variants in the field, although the highly classified nature of those operatives has relegated such conversation to the realm of speculation.

Due to its proven performance, the Ordnance Commission has provided an exception for this GEN1 system.

STATISTICS

MANUFACTURER
Materials Group

LOCATION
Damascus, Vhalkem, CHI CETI IV

TESTING SITE
SWC, Songnam

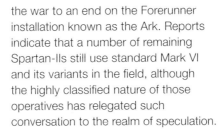

Classic GEN1 heads-up display schema

Solid collar frame and branch-locking system

Class-3B Essen shield distributor

Brightly colored armor often differentiates teams during War Games training exercises.

OCEANIC

MJOLNIR POWERED ASSAULT ARMOR [GEN2] - OCEANIC

When the United Rebel Front's scattered remnants coalesced on the hydroelectric platforms distributed across the water world of Terceira, a number of "wake siege specialists" were deployed to take it back. Many of these operators utilized Hannibal Weapon Systems' OCEANIC-class armor, a GEN2 Mjolnir variant specifically intended to be used in aphotic, deep-sea scenarios, where pressure and temperature threaten to slow and crush standard armor systems. Although aphotic operations are rare, the OCEANIC-class has proven itself to be extremely useful outside the water as well and has also been deployed near artificial gravity wells and conduction-intensive fields.

OCEANIC is arguably the most resilient Mjolnir armor system in the current GEN2 stable.

STATISTICS

MANUFACTURER
Hannibal Weapon Systems

LOCATION
Kotka, Pori, NEW CARTHAGE

TESTING SITE
WG/Facility 93-00/Kotka

Pressure-resistant cross-brace on visor

Posterior lock for modular pressure shroud

Anterior lock for modular pressure shroud

Peel-casing pauldron to streamline movement in particle-dense environments

Due to its cost, operation of this armor requires level-four Ordnance Commission approval.

ORBITAL

MJOLNIR POWERED ASSAULT ARMOR [GEN2] - ORBITAL

A modified variant following the same production lines as EVA, the armor known as ORBITAL was developed to specifically cater to orbital and suborbital combat, where conditions similar to space often converge with harsh atmospheric and gravity-borne challenges. ORBITAL saw extensive testing during the final battles of the

Covenant War, when the alien collective assaulted the Sol system. It was during those battles that ORBITAL-class armor was deployed to secure and defend the skyhooks and tethers above Earth, Luna, and Mars. This test, and the success it brought, would lead to ORBITAL's pervasive adoption among Spartan-IVs.

STATISTICS

MANUFACTURER
Naphtali Contractor Corporation

LOCATION
Abilene, North America, EARTH

TESTING SITE
Buffalo Breaker Yards

It remains to be seen if adoption of ORBITAL systems will ever eclipse EVA.

War Games tests have proven ORBITAL's viability repeatedly.

"Mark of the Breaker," was the first armor to have survived the legendary Buffalo Breaker Yards

Momentum-governing collar mounts

Buffalo A-29 comm suite

Tow-grip isolation case for stabilized mobility

PROTECTOR

MJOLNIR POWERED ASSAULT ARMOR [GEN2] - PROTECTOR

After the Covenant War, the Materials Group dispersed a number of their existing combat armor contracts to other materiel production companies and internally spearheaded a new focus on defense optimization systems. Their most prominent armor within this category is easily PROTECTOR, a heavy-rated, anti-infiltration, and siege-resistant armor system that offers incredible resiliency and resourcefulness for defensive stands, predominantly within large population centers and urban environments. PROTECTOR has served in a number of capacities since its inception, the most notable being the raids of Mindoro and Volamon on the colony of Cascade.

STATISTICS

MANUFACTURER
Materials Group

LOCATION
Damascus, Vhalkem, CHI CETI IV

TESTING SITE
Damascus Testing Facility

Interlocking firm-plate visor, including multiple sensor relays

Narrow-set fusion harness

Sealed Muroto charge piston

PROTECTOR is optimized for zone defensive positions and forward plane coverage.

The Muroto charge piston enhances the operator's reactive stability, improving weapon use.

RAIDER-class armor saw increased usage in War Games simulations, specifically within Oddball competitions.

930-AV4 Class-2 Ankara tactical assault suite

Accession pauldron conduit for in-field modifications

Eccentric, feral design to intimidate adversaries

Standard GEN2 titanium nanocomposite mesh

STATISTICS

MANUFACTURER
Imbrium Machine Complex

LOCATION
Ankara, Mare Imbrium, LUNA

TESTING SITE
Anakara Resiliency Chamber

RAIDER

MJOLNIR POWERED ASSAULT ARMOR [GEN2] - RAIDER

There are very few Mjolnir variants with this degree of architectural eccentricity and elaboration, physically designed to undermine and disorient the mental faculties of enemy forces. Imbrium Machine Complex readily affirms that the feral and exotic look of RAIDER-class armor has one very simple purpose: To agitate enemy response sufficiently enough to slow down reaction times, thereby making the opposition vulnerable to attack. This methodology is not new, however, as it was first observed during the early years of the SPARTAN-II project, when rebel forces were confronted with soldiers who appeared to be inhuman.

Focusing on operation singularity, RANGER-class armor is not architecturally comparable to any other Mjolnir system.

Low-display bifocal visor balances intel management over visibility

Resilient atmosphere inductors line helmet

Energy shield 7P-LCF actuator plug components

Low-set concave pauldron design offers impressive resiliency

STATISTICS

MANUFACTURER
Imbrium Machine Complex

LOCATION
Ankara, Mare Imbrium, LUNA

TESTING SITE
Anakara Resiliency Chamber

RANGER

MJOLNIR POWERED ASSAULT ARMOR [GEN2] - RANGER

Most contemporary armor systems on Mjolnir's production line are optimized for team functionality and designed for use withi a squad-based element. A handful, however, have been engineered for single-combatant effectiveness, where Spartan operators are deployed into the field on their own, independent of not only a standard fireteam but also of intel cache, support handlers, and mission controllers. Imbrium Machine Complex's RANGER-class armor is, without a doubt, the leader within this armor subset, with its early prototypes rumored to have infiltrated the Covenant homeworld of High Charity in the latter years of the war.

RECON

MJOLNIR POWERED ASSAULT ARMOR [GEN2] - RECON

Previously manufactured by the Materials Group based out of Swanbourne, RECON has historically been one of the more prominent Mjolnir systems, often employed by force scouting and reconnaissance teams. After the Ordnance Commission in May of 2553, Imbrium Machine Complex took control of oversight and production for RECON-class systems, refining and improving the existing architecture for use by SPARTAN-IV personnel. While the physical shape of the armor has retained its classic, low-profile symmetry, most operators indicate that it bears a notably higher resiliency and a much leaner reaction-time margin, both of which present obvious advantages in the field.

STATISTICS

MANUFACTURER
Imbrium Machine Complex

LOCATION
Ankara, Mare Imbrium, LUNA

TESTING SITE
Anakara Resiliency Chamber

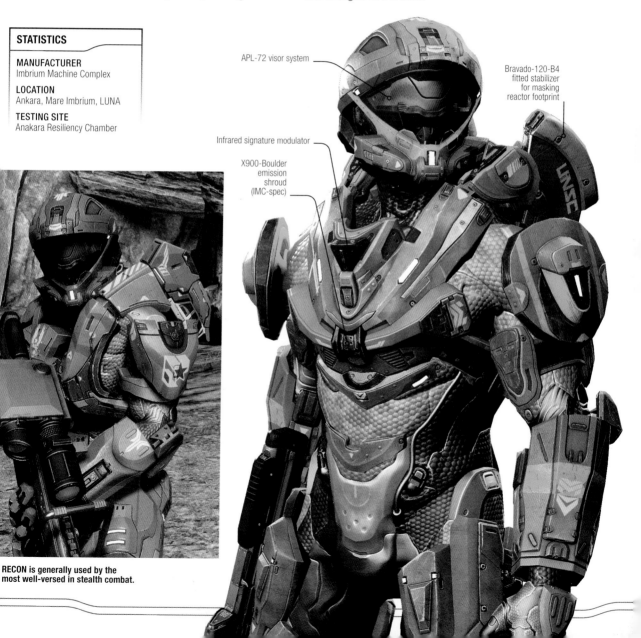

APL-72 visor system

Bravado-120-B4 fitted stabilizer for masking reactor footprint

Infrared signature modulator

X900-Boulder emission shroud (IMC-spec)

RECON is generally used by the most well-versed in stealth combat.

Despite RECRUIT's base feature set, its performance consistency still raises eyebrows, even among the more experienced.

STATISTICS

MANUFACTURER
Hannibal Weapon Systems

LOCATION
Kotka, Pori, NEW CARTHAGE

TESTING SITE
WG/Facility 93-00/Kotka

Base VISR 4.0 heads-up display integration

Class-A hardened reactor case

Common solid-plate pauldron

Standard ceramic folds allowing flow-mobility

RECRUIT

MJOLNIR POWERED ASSAULT ARMOR [GEN2] - RECRUIT

The default armor configuration for recently inducted SPARTAN-IV personnel is the well-known RECRUIT-class system. This standard suit is designed to cope with the strain and duress experienced by newly augmented super-soldiers in the field, as dictated by the classic ORION protocols of the late 25th century. Despite its popularity, many Spartans eventually opt to diversify their preferred system, creating an armor set unique to their skills and abilities. In the interim, however, RECRUIT provides a healthy foundation to build on, encompassing the capacity and limitations of all contemporary armor systems as they are experienced in the field.

SCOUT

MJOLNIR POWERED ASSAULT ARMOR [GEN2] - SCOUT

STATISTICS

MANUFACTURER
Materials Group

LOCATION
Swanbourne, Australia, EARTH

TESTING SITE
WG/Facility 58-32/B5D

For several decades, Forward Deployed Operators (FDO) have been crucial to all areas of force recon determination, specifically as it pertains to Spartan operations. The SCOUT-class armor is the only Mjolnir system that has consistently been favored by FDOs, probably because of its incredibly capable covert anti-tracking systems and shroud-induction packages. These subsystems allow personnel operating SCOUT armor to effectively navigate the battlefield without generating a recognizable silhouette on enemy sensors, even within the most challenging and harried of circumstances.

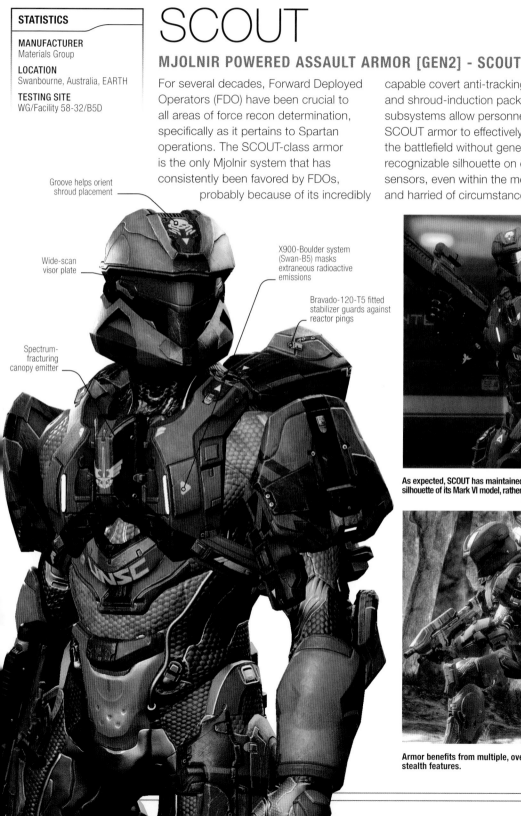

Groove helps orient shroud placement

Wide-scan visor plate

Spectrum-fracturing canopy emitter

X900-Boulder system (Swan-B5) masks extraneous radioactive emissions

Bravado-120-T5 fitted stabilizer guards against reactor pings

As expected, SCOUT has maintained the basic GEN1 silhouette of its Mark VI model, rather than its earlier Mark V.

Armor benefits from multiple, overlapping stealth features.

SOLDIER maintains the second highest armor adoption rate on the UNSC *Infinity*.

"Team endurance catalyst" intel suite

Helmet components are similar to those used by Marines

Standard GEN2 titanium nanocomposite mesh

Variable case structure, which extends combat sustainability

STATISTICS

MANUFACTURER
Materials Group

LOCATION
Damascus, Vhalkem, CHI CETI IV

TESTING SITE
Damascus Testing Facility

SOLDIER

MJOLNIR POWERED ASSAULT ARMOR [GEN2] - SOLDIER

Using a SOLDIER-class armor system, personnel are able to physically carry more equipment, materiel, and ammunition, with minimal disruption of their critical motor functionality and speed. This generally means that the role most common for SOLDIER-clad Spartans is that of support and engineering, but it does not constitute their only role, or indicate that such Spartans are relegated as ancillary. Spartans wearing SOLDIER-class armor systems can efficiently function in any role and are particularly lethal due to their ability to resourcefully endure long and protracted firefights well beyond other Spartans.

VANGUARD

MJOLNIR POWERED ASSAULT ARMOR [GEN2] - VANGUARD

Used by Hannibal Weapon Systems as a test bed for a large majority of their prototype technologies, VANGUARD-class is a streamlined armor system designed solely for enemy engagement. What this effectively means is that VANGUARD's singular purpose is not dependent on supplemental factors, such as reconnaissance, communication, or materiel-specific optimization, but rather only on components that immediately benefit combat ability. HWS leverages improvements to movement, battle methodology, and action management, not only vetting them for cross-variant integration but also simply adding to VANGUARD's existing formidability.

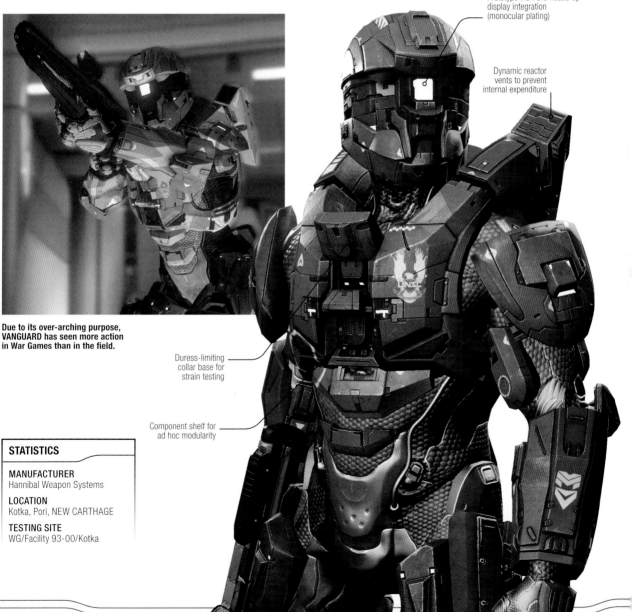

Due to its over-arching purpose, VANGUARD has seen more action in War Games than in the field.

Prototype VISR 5.0 heads-up display integration (monocular plating)

Dynamic reactor vents to prevent internal expenditure

Duress-limiting collar base for strain testing

Component shelf for ad hoc modularity

STATISTICS

MANUFACTURER
Hannibal Weapon Systems

LOCATION
Kotka, Pori, NEW CARTHAGE

TESTING SITE
WG/Facility 93-00/Kotka

Spatial recognition
functionality

Full-mobility,
overclocking
movement
packages

Embedded, minimal silhouette
pauldrons for improved
close-quarters combat

Unlike CQB before it, VENATOR is immediately solvent for both close-quarters and long-range combat.

VENATOR

MJOLNIR POWERED ASSAULT ARMOR [GEN2] - VENATOR

True to the form of most classical Close-Quarters Battle (CQB) systems, VENATOR-class armor optimizes mobility, speed, and flexibility within the context of hand-to-hand encounters. Designed by Concord's Lethbridge Industrial, many advocate VENATOR as the full realization of CQB's time-honored methodology of overclocking functionality packages, which allows operators to push their armor well beyond recommended mobility settings, usually resulting in remarkable combat performance at close range. Most extraordinary is the armor's spatial recognition functionality, actively providing responsive improvements based on the operator's immediate surroundings.

WAR MASTER

MJOLNIR POWERED ASSAULT ARMOR [GEN2] - WAR MASTER

Where VANGUARD-class armor utilizes streamlined functionality that focuses specifically on combat effectiveness, WAR MASTER lies on the opposite end of that spectrum, offering possibly the broadest versatility for all armor types. Considered the most exotic Mjolnir system manufactured by Lethbridge Industrial, WAR MASTER-class armor matches the rugged

resiliency of heavy variants with the speed and dexterity of light variants, including a full communications suite, networked sensors, and remote deployment componentry. This makes its functionality incredibly expansive, no matter what its purpose.

Fear around potentially overextended performance specs has abated since WAR MASTER hit the field.

Visor contours are intended to intimidate enemies

R-42 case-filter rebreather

Shield recoupler (Corsica-102) improves armor resiliency

Plane-reactor coupling increases mobility through weight distribution

Low-set pauldrons lend themselves to operator variability

STATISTICS

MANUFACTURER
Lethbridge Industrial

LOCATION
Lethbridge, Corsica, CONCORD

TESTING SITE
Lethbridge Combat Fields

WARRIOR

MJOLNIR POWERED ASSAULT ARMOR [GEN2] - WARRIOR

During the transition from GEN1 to GEN2, the Materials Group focused one specific armor template on optimizing speed and mobility, even at the cost of overall combat effectiveness. The outcome of this venture eventually became the WARRIOR-class armor—a system that increases reaction time and softens joint duress on overexertion, giving the Spartan access to full mobility without the limitations customary with most Mjolnir variants. Despite this solution being well-received by Spartans, the Materials Group has cautioned that discretion be used while operating this armor, since misuse can result in extreme injuries and even death.

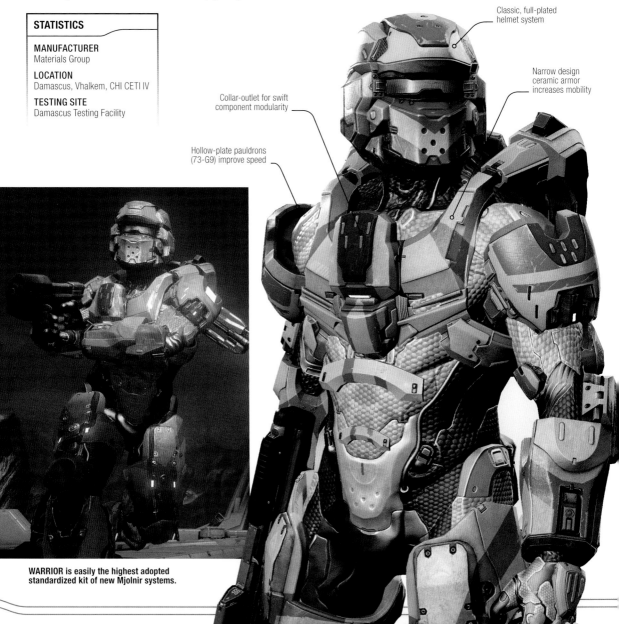

STATISTICS

MANUFACTURER
Materials Group

LOCATION
Damascus, Vhalkem, CHI CETI IV

TESTING SITE
Damascus Testing Facility

Classic, full-plated helmet system

Narrow design ceramic armor increases mobility

Collar-outlet for swift component modularity

Hollow-plate pauldrons (73-G9) improve speed

WARRIOR is easily the highest adopted standardized kit of new Mjolnir systems.

Simply stated, WETWORK is designed to kill.

WETWORK

MJOLNIR POWERED ASSAULT ARMOR [GEN2] - WETWORK

WETWORK's lack of profile in Spartan populations isn't due to its quality, but rather its necessity. Lethbridge Industrial designed WETWORK-class armor to only be employed during highly-classified target acquisition or elimination scenarios, a requirement that sets it apart from all other combat systems. Within this peculiar distinction, WETWORK's technology is most critical when high-value enemies must be removed on an individual basis and with extreme discretion. During the civil revolts on Talitsa, WETWORK was instrumental in stemming the growing dissidence in the colony's largest population centers by swiftly and delicately eliminating the leadership of several uprisings.

Linear target-focused visor architecture

Long-range impact layers for collecting vibrations and sound over great distances

Sub-collar plate contacts for stealth modifications

Anterior flex-locked hard points for equipment

WETWORK's operability was tested in the heavily restricted territory called the Lethbridge Combat Fields.

STATISTICS

MANUFACTURER
Lethbridge Industrial

LOCATION
Lethbridge, Corsica, CONCORD

TESTING SITE
Lethbridge Combat Fields

OPERATOR systems saw the most usage toward the end of the Covenant War.

STATISTICS

MANUFACTURER
Naphtali Contractor Corporation

LOCATION
Abilene, North America, EARTH

TESTING SITE
Buffalo Breaker Yards

Open visor view-plate for increased range of spectrum

Dual-locked rebreather (PV-20) generally worn by pilots

External harness bracers

Twin-release cables route energy expenditure to reserve systems

OPERATOR

MJOLNIR POWERED ASSAULT ARMOR [GEN2] - OPERATOR

Existing throughout nearly all of Mjolnir's GEN1 series, OPERATOR-class armor was designed to benefit personnel who were engaged in unconventional warfare, and more specifically the Beta-Five Division's AAG (Asymmetrical Action Group). When Chalybs Defense Solutions fell prey to the Covenant's assault on Meridian, Earth's Naphtali Contractor Corporation acquired the armor system and began spearheading designs for the GEN2 version. And it was in the derelict shipyard just outside the city of Abilene, the renowned testing site referred to as the "Buffalo Breaker Yards," that the NCC finalized the design and substance of the new OPERATOR-class armor.

PIONEER

MJOLNIR POWERED ASSAULT ARMOR [GEN2] - PIONEER

STATISTICS

MANUFACTURER
Acheron Security

LOCATION
Gdynia, Acheron Fossae, MARS

TESTING SITE
Acheron Trauma Sim

With a recent impetus behind the Unified Earth Government's pioneer initiative in order to claim new territories for human colonization, Acheron Security set aside a budget and design team to specifically address security concerns for such endeavors. Within a number of months, PIONEER-class armor was presented as an optimal security solution for expeditions of this nature. In the time since its production, PIONEER's usage has been incredibly profound, assisting in the security and protection of over two dozen field teams and science detachments. Its most notable usage, however, was during the highly-classified exploration efforts on Installation 03 by Ivanoff Station's research deployments.

Passive, redundant environmental scanners

Dual-locked rebreather (YV-65) leveraged in hostile environments

Twin-plated visual sensor for increased range of spectrum

PNR-S7 Split-convex pauldron

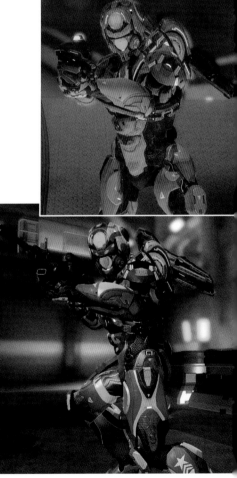

PIONEER-class armor has often been leveraged to guard science teams on colonization operations, and even to protect planetary engineering rigs.

IMC's work with PATHFINDER has broken numerous challenge-duration records, particularly during its brutal stints in Luna's legendary Black Forest.

Self-actuated, independent intel assessing systems

Heavy-gauge atmosphere filtration vents

IMBR-119 Close-fitting pauldron units to allow smooth mobility in dense foliage

PATHFINDER

MJOLNIR POWERED ASSAULT ARMOR [GEN2] - PATHFINDER

Imbrium Machine Complex's most rigorously tested piece of military equipment, PATHFINDER-class armor was made to withstand excessively challenging conditions in hostile terrain, even for prolonged lengths of time. PATHFINDER effectively allows Spartan personnel to endure well outside of anticipated parameters and life expectancy ratios. IMC leveraged the nearby Bosque de Negro ("Black Forest") to determine the overall viability of this armor, individually deploying a number of PATHFINDER-equipped Spartans into the heart of this territory without any equipment or outside contact. Remarkably, these Spartans not only survived but thrived, forging their way through the forest's deadly terrain and wildlife.

Upper cuisse plate

ENGINEER

MJOLNIR POWERED ASSAULT ARMOR [GEN2] - ENGINEER

When it comes to the military application of equipment infiltration, subversion, and reconstitution, there is no other Mjolnir system that is better suited for it than Lethbridge Industrial's ENGINEER-class armor. While it was not fully explored until years into the war, the reapplication and usage of Covenant assets in the field was instrumental in guiding the early design of ENGINEER. This armor was first deployed onto the volatile moon of Thales to halt criminal activity in the colony's docking complexes, and it would later see action during Spartan-IV operations on the Forerunner world of Requiem.

STATISTICS

MANUFACTURER
Lethbridge Industrial

LOCATION
Lethbridge, Corsica, CONCORD

TESTING SITE
Lethbridge Combat Fields

Quad-set spectrum nodes loosely resemble Huragok eye placement

Assessment locator module (LW-210) used to lock onto machine irregularities

Pack-mounted release grip to govern energy reappropriation

Despite its overriding functional purpose, ENGINEER is still impressive in combat.

Componential shield redistributor cartridge mounted onto the collar for easy modification

With only a handful in active operation at any given time, ENGINEER is often considered to be the rarest combat armor system.

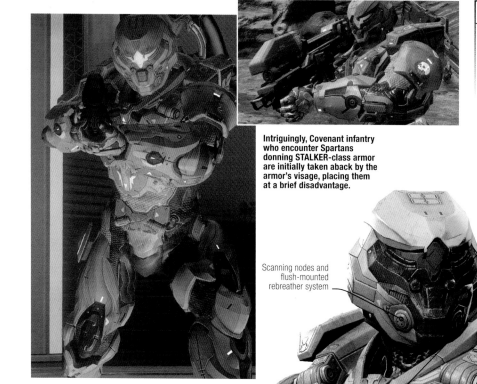

STATISTICS

MANUFACTURER
Naphtali Contractor Corporation

LOCATION
Abilene, North America, EARTH

TESTING SITE
Buffalo Breaker Yards

Intriguingly, Covenant infantry who encounter Spartans donning STALKER-class armor are initially taken aback by the armor's visage, placing them at a brief disadvantage.

Irregular beam visor is loosely based on Jiralhanae "Stalker" visor schema

Horizontal, cross-set shield conduits

Scanning nodes and flush-mounted rebreather system

STALKER

MJOLNIR POWERED ASSAULT ARMOR [GEN2] - STALKER

After the UNSC first encountered Jiralhanae special forces, informally dubbed "Brute Stalkers," efforts were undertaken to acquire and reverse engineer their distributed technology for practical hunter-tracker field application. After some research, it became clear that only a loose interpretation of the exotic architecture could be applied to UNSC systems effectively, largely due to its eccentric nature. Naphtali Contractor Corporation took advantage of this intel, optimizing a variant of Mjolnir called STALKER-class armor, which integrated Jiralhanae stealth and hunter systems, including numerous other separate advancements made by ONI.

ROGUE

MJOLNIR POWERED ASSAULT ARMOR [GEN2] - ROGUE

The destruction of several critical materiel production colonies demanded that other worlds fill their roles, as was the case with Vestol Corporation's GEN1 ROGUE-class armor based out of the now-glassed world of Tribute. Shortly after Vestol's extant assets were liquidated, Hannibal Weapon Systems acquired a number of patents for military reapplication, including approval from the Ordnance Commission to explore ROGUE-class armor for GEN2 integration. Although early tests were curious and unorthodox in the years that followed, the standard ROGUE-class variant deployed by HWS three years after was roundly accepted and regarded as superior to the systems that came before.

STATISTICS

MANUFACTURER
Hannibal Weapon Systems

LOCATION
Kotka, Pori, NEW CARTHAGE

TESTING SITE
WG/Facility 93-00/Kotka

In War Games' free-for-all modes, ROGUE remains one of the most successful, because of its lack of reliance on customary team standards.

Multi-plate, heavy angled layout offers single operators improved intel

Extensively increased FOV from GEN1 variant

Modular U6-9 rebreathers are set high on the jaw for protection

Sub-collar, under-locking shield emitter

TRACKER

MJOLNIR POWERED ASSAULT ARMOR [GEN2] - TRACKER

In the late 2200s, off-world tracking became particularly important both for locating fugitives who had fled a world and shadowing potential suspects across an entire star system. Recognizing the necessity for this technology in combat, Acheron Security developed TRACKER-class armor specifically designed to assist personnel in locating and following targets across incredibly long distances, including both interplanetary and interstellar spaces. The TRACKER-class suite includes satellite link feeds, persistent silhouette-locking agents, and cloud-induction tracers—all of which allow Spartans to track and shadow targets over great spans and with extremely narrow line-of-sight margins.

STATISTICS

MANUFACTURER
Acheron Security

LOCATION
Gdynia, Acheron Fossae, MARS

TESTING SITE
Acheron Trauma Sim

Anti-flare vision shroud covers nodes

Tricloptic node cluster improves target tracking

Strain-resistant reactor case to mitigate gravity-induced trauma

Energy stack funnel that dynamically adjusts shield resilience

TRACKER-clad Spartans were indispensable in locating specific Covenant commanders across Requiem's many sites.

Although designed for extreme-range sniping, DEADEYE still offers considerable functionality at both mid- and close-range.

STATISTICS

MANUFACTURER
Hannibal Weapon Systems

LOCATION
Kotka, Pori, NEW CARTHAGE

TESTING SITE
Tribute's ship graveyard

Point-isolation, VISR focal software used for extreme-range targeting

Standard reactor case

Enclosed PZ-238 rebreather system

DEADEYE

MJOLNIR POWERED ASSAULT ARMOR [GEN2] - DEADEYE

Rare in the field but highly regarded by its advocates, DEADEYE-class armor was created by Hannibal Weapon Systems for long-range target purging, filling out the extreme end of sniper-optimized Spartan armor. Through smart-linked VISR software with movement-distance calibration, DEADEYE has been updated to assist snipers at ranges that greatly exceed traditional firing accuracy. To vet the system prior to full production, HWS tested DEADEYE within the vast debris field hanging above the northern pole of Tribute, deploying Spartans in zero-gravity to affect long-range combat against exoatmospheric drones hidden among the wreckage.

LOCUS' unconventional design has ironically increased its popularity.

LOCUS

MJOLNIR POWERED ASSAULT ARMOR [GEN2] - LOCUS

LOCUS-class armor was designed for enemy fortification ingress scenarios with the focus on survivability and durability. Unlike other infiltration-based armor systems, Lethbridge Industrial wanted to ensure its resiliency in combat, in addition to its attention to stealth and anti-security measures. LOCUS was tested just outside the megacity of Lethbridge on the planet Concord, in a number of heavily secured facilities lying across Corsica's hardscrabble northern outskirts. These tests proved unequivocally that LOCUS-class armor was not only competent at infiltration scenarios, but also fully capable of surviving extreme opposition and firepower.

Heavily armored case-locked visor system relies on multiple visual feeds

Interlocking helmet soft-mesh loosely based on Covenant armor technology

R4-100 open-dial audio sensors used for noise tracking

STATISTICS

MANUFACTURER
Lethbridge Industrial

LOCATION
Lethbridge, Corsica, CONCORD

TESTING SITE
Lethbridge Combat Fields

SCANNER

MJOLNIR POWERED ASSAULT ARMOR [GEN2] - SCANNER

When the Office of Naval Intelligence commissioned SCANNER-class armor, it was based on concerns around high profile persons, specifically military leaders, being captured by enemy forces. In the case of such losses, ONI wanted to have Spartan fireteams outfitted specifically for search-and-rescue operations and SCANNER-class armor effectively meets this end. The Materials Group, based out of Chi Ceti IV, worked several years on balancing the needs of such personnel, appropriately fine-tuning individual components like long-range sensors and larger toolsets like armor-fixed rescue implements—the SCANNER-class system is the remarkable culmination of such work.

STATISTICS

MANUFACTURER
Materials Group

LOCATION
Damascus, Vhalkem, CHI CETI IV

TESTING SITE
Damascus Testing Facility

LCX-20V1 SinoViet sight-augmentation module for extreme-range reconnaissance

Low-set, concave rebreather apparatus

SCANNER's SV module doesn't mitigate operability in standard combat, and can even be slid back into a passive mode above the operator's parietal plate.

Few systems can boast sensory effectiveness of SCANNER.

STRIDER

MJOLNIR POWERED ASSAULT ARMOR [GEN2] - STRIDER

Prior to the war with the Covenant, the notion of "jaunt-combat excursions" was not considered relevant or practically viable, but such conclusions have changed dramatically. In UNSC engagements, the term "Strider" typically encompasses the activity of operators committing to a number of highly varied missions over an extremely short period of time (usually just hours) and within an isolated military campaign. Imbrium Machine Complex's STRIDER-class armor offers greater overall endurance than most Mjolnir systems, handily resolving multi-task aggregation, coordinating missions on the fly, and effectually giving the operating Spartans the solvency needed to execute accordingly.

STATISTICS

MANUFACTURER
Imbrium Machine Complex

LOCATION
Ankara, Mare Imbrium, LUNA

TESTING SITE
Anakara Resiliency Chamber

Spartans equipped with STRIDER often utilize jet packs to increase mobility during the course of an excursion.

Closed-breach secondary sensor components open at operator's request

Standard RECRUIT-system utilized for cost optimization

Ankara EV-A760 wide-range visor set

Twin-case Class-8 support module (KR-03-A) used to improve survivability in space

STRIDER's ability to quickly and deftly adapt to battlefield changes make it optimal for JCE scenarios.

Standard RECRUIT-class abdomen plate

FOTUS armor was extensively tested in Kirkland's overcast and frigid nine-month winter season.

Torque-node component used to distract nearby predators

Base detects levels of gravity-trough scaturiency

Extended awareness conduit (ALK-03) heightens mobility around senior operatives and moving-equipment personnel

Lodged-tracking component 793-VF for improved survivability and maintenance

FOTUS

MJOLNIR POWERED ASSAULT ARMOR [GEN2] - FOTUS

Composited from loose Forerunner technology that was merged with base Mjolnir architecture, the long-rumored FOTUS armor set was initially forged in the RTC Facility before being transported to the Willows Complex for durability and survivability testing. Initial runs went well, but prior to the Kirkland plant moving forward to full production, the armor's engineers required that it met COUGAR-class safety protocols in an effort to protect it against feral branches of local wildlife. After protocols were met, FOTUS-class systems were deployed in the field and most often used to acquire coffee at a variety of lightly secured sites, during the town's long seasons of wet, freezing cold weather.

90-RZ java-fuel monitoring software evaluates current sustainability levels

STATISTICS

MANUFACTURER
343 Industries

LOCATION
Kirkland, North America, EARTH

TESTING SITE
434 Combat Readiness Lab

SHIPS

UNSC FORWARD UNTO DAWN

CHARON-CLASS LIGHT FRIGATE

The UNSC frigate known as *Forward Unto Dawn* served on the frontlines during the final days of the Covenant War and is well-distinguished for its pursuit of Covenant forces through the Forerunner portal at Voi. After defeating the Covenant, *Dawn* attempted to flee the firing of a local Halo ring, only to be severed into two, sending part of the ship back to Earth. The other part, which held the living legend known as the Master Chief and his AI Cortana, absently floated in uncharted space for years, until finally being pulled into the mysterious Forerunner world of Requiem.

A holographic display indicates the *Dawn*'s perilous state.

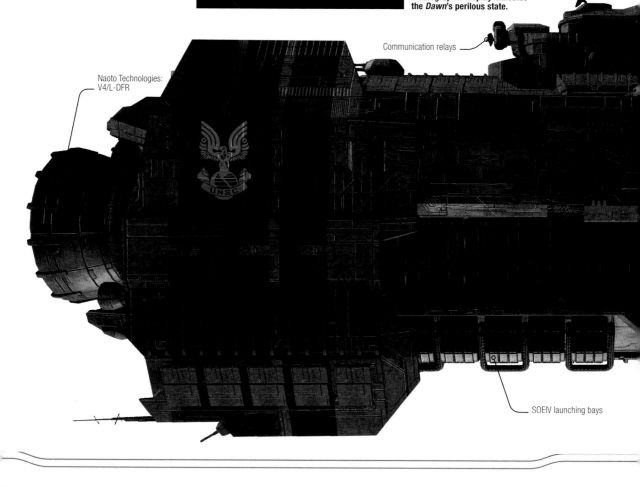

Communication relays

Naoto Technologies:
V4/L-DFR

SOEIV launching bays

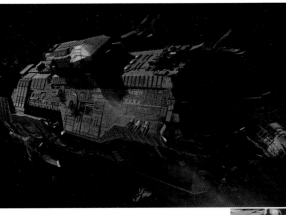

When the Ark's portal collapsed, the *Dawn* was severed into two.

Dawn maintained three Hyperion nuclear missile silos in a large bay near its observation deck.

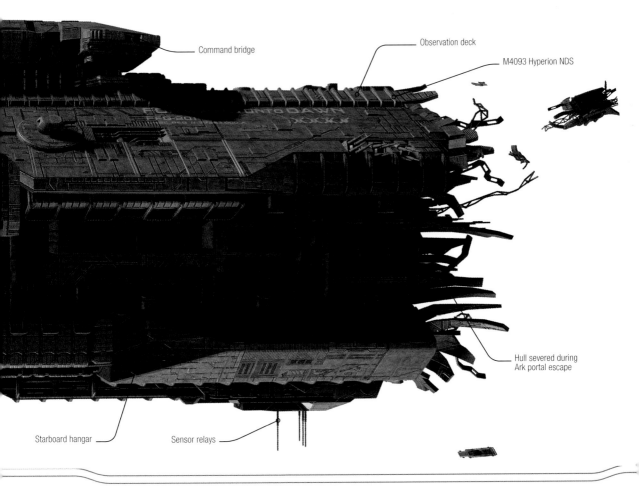

Command bridge

Observation deck

M4093 Hyperion NDS

Hull severed during Ark portal escape

Starboard hangar

Sensor relays

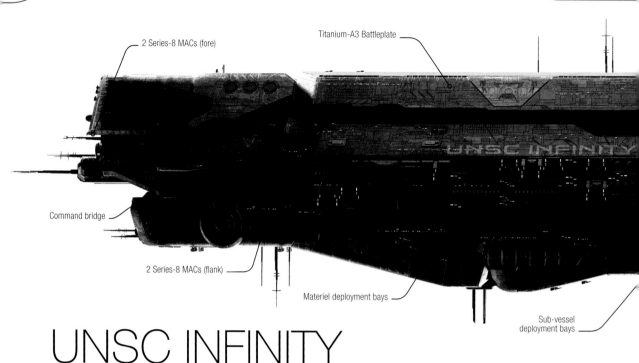

2 Series-8 MACs (fore)

Titanium-A3 Battleplate

Command bridge

2 Series-8 MACs (flank)

Materiel deployment bays

Sub-vessel
deployment bays

UNSC INFINITY

INFINITY-CLASS STARSHIP

Without equal throughout all of UNSC's naval forces, *Infinity* is the largest and most powerful vessel ever employed by humanity. It was designed prior to the end of the war to contend with the Covenant—something the Navy had failed to do effectively for almost thirty years. After 2552, *Infinity* was publicly commissioned for peaceful exploration and research, but this would change when its crew came upon Requiem and was mercilessly pulled into its shielded outer surface. After managing to escape, *Infinity* returned several months later under the leadership of Captain Thomas Lasky, and once again contended with the forces of Requiem.

STATISTICS

REGISTRY
INF-101

LENGTH
18,682ft (5,694m)

BEAM
2,734ft (833m)

HEIGHT
3,416ft (1,041m)

PRIMARY ARMAMENT
CR-03, Series-8 MAC

SECONDARY ARMAMENT
M42 Archer Missile Delivery System

TERTIARY ARMAMENT
M75 Rapier Missile Delivery System

QUATERNARY ARMAMENT
M96 Howler Missile Delivery System

QUINARY ARMAMENT
M965 Fortress 70mm Point Defense Network

ENGINE ROOM

Infinity was originally designed for war, but its commissioning ceremony rechristened it for peace—though that would not last.

Memorial Park atrium

XR2 Boglin Fields
Sublight Engine

Primary science decks

Spartan Town

During the Didact's attack on Earth, *Infinity* engaged *Mantle's Approach*, despite the Forerunner vessel's incredible size.

STATISTICS

CLASS PICTURED
Sahara (Heavy Prowler)

CLASS LENGTH
922ft (281m)

CLASS BEAM
509ft (155m)

CLASS HEIGHT
203ft (62m)

PRIMARY ARMAMENT
XEV9-Matos Nonlinear Pulse Cannons

SECONDARY ARMAMENT
M947 Shiva Nuclear Delivery System

TERTIARY ARMAMENT
M441 Hornet Remote Explosive System

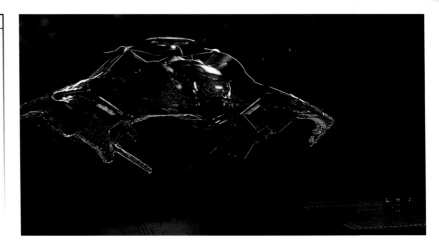

ONI's *Aladdin* is a *Sahara*-class prowler and is significantly larger than other prowler classes.

ONI PROWLER

WINTER, RAZOR, ECLIPSE, AND SAHARA CLASSES

Prowlers are high-impact, low-profile variants of the UNSC's classic corvette design, used almost exclusively for stealth and reconnaissance missions, though some exceptions have been noted. Prior to the war, prowlers did not utilize extremely effective active camouflage systems, but after reverse-engineering assets stolen from the Covenant, this all changed—all contemporary prowlers now incorporate some form of hull camouflage technology. ONI sometimes leverages the prowlers' concealment systems to facilitate a number of internal operations, including the deployment of classified black ops groups and the transportation of high-level commanders, or even prisoners.

Long-range tactical sensors

Active sensor array

Command bridge

Ablative hull composite shrouds presence

XEV9-Matos Cannons

Under-carriage docking bay

M947 Shiva NDS

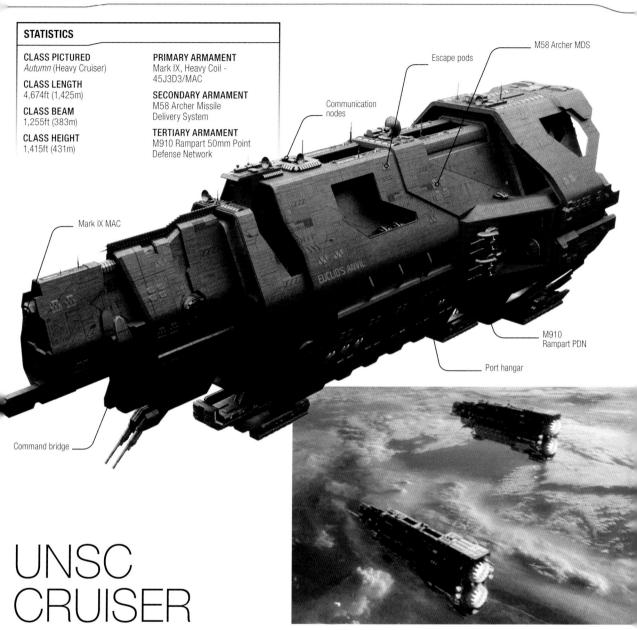

STATISTICS

CLASS PICTURED
Autumn (Heavy Cruiser)

CLASS LENGTH
4,674ft (1,425m)

CLASS BEAM
1,255ft (383m)

CLASS HEIGHT
1,415ft (431m)

PRIMARY ARMAMENT
Mark IX, Heavy Coil -
45J3D3/MAC

SECONDARY ARMAMENT
M58 Archer Missile
Delivery System

TERTIARY ARMAMENT
M910 Rampart 50mm Point
Defense Network

Escape pods

M58 Archer MDS

Communication
nodes

Mark IX MAC

M910
Rampart PDN

Port hangar

Command bridge

Autumn-class vessels are heavy cruisers, but also provide escort support when needed.

UNSC CRUISER

HALCYON, MARATHON, VALIANT, AND AUTUMN CLASSES

At the start of the war, the UNSC's two most prolific cruiser classes were *Halcyon* and *Marathon*. Interestingly, neither of these classes survived the war unscathed—most *Halcyon*-class cruisers were decommissioned during the final years of the war with the *Marathon*-class following shortly behind, with only a handful remaining in service. A last ditch effort to rend

the Covenant's control of Reach, however, created the legendary *Pillar of Autumn*, a heavily modified *Halcyon*-class cruiser refit specifically for Operation: RED FLAG in 2552. While the *Autumn* would be destroyed on Halo later, its numerous upgrades were highly regaled and inspired the *Autumn*-class cruiser, helping to further augment the UNSC's post-war Navy.

Strident-class frigates are incredibly versatile, capable of being deployed as lone sentries above ONI research facilities or as swift attack vessels during large-scale naval conflicts.

UNSC FRIGATE

STALWART, CHARON, PARIS, AND STRIDENT CLASSES

Easily one of the most critical vessels within the UNSC Navy during the course of the war, humanity's frigates are light combat ships designed for speed, maneuverability, and firepower. The most recent addition to the frigate type is the *Strident*-class, lean and lethal machines, which pack incredible firepower. They include a Mark IV ship-mounted MAC and three Hyperion nuclear warheads—weapons capable of easily downing a variety of Covenant capital ships. In fact, *Strident*-class frigates are considered so invaluable that even the enormous and powerful UNSC *Infinity* carries a number of them, underslung within its sub-vessel deployment bay. After an initial assault, these are deployed en masse, delivering a final, crushing blow and mopping up any stragglers in the process. Without question, frigates remain at the center of the UNSC's naval dominance in the years following the Covenant War.

STATISTICS

CLASS PICTURED
Strident (Heavy Frigate)

CLASS LENGTH
1,887ft (575m)

CLASS BEAM
407ft (124m)

CLASS HEIGHT
368ft (112m)

PRIMARY ARMAMENT
Mark IV, Heavy Coil - 94B1E6/MAC

SECONDARY ARMAMENT
M42 Archer Missile Delivery System

TERTIARY ARMAMENT
M870 Rampart 50mm Point Defense Network

QUATERNARY ARMAMENT
M4093 Hyperion Nuclear Delivery System

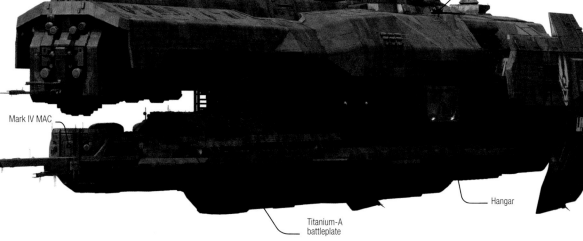

Command bridge

M4093 Hyperion NDS

M870 Rampart 50mm PDN

Mark IV MAC

Hangar

Titanium-A battleplate

MANTLE'S APPROACH

PROMETHEAN COMMAND WARSHIP

Designed during the ancient conflict with humanity, the Didact's personal warship, *Mantle's Approach*, was a Forerunner vessel without equal. Though not nearly as large as many other Forerunner ships, *Approach* was generally unmatched in both speed and armament. *Mantle's Approach* would also be the site of the Librarian's final betrayal of the Didact and she would seal it away on Requiem, hoping that upon her husband's awakening, he would use it wisely. This, however, did not happen—the Didact, still consumed by his hatred for humanity, used the ship to assault the planet Earth. Nevertheless, it would be destroyed by a nuclear weapon in the hands of the Master Chief.

STATISTICS

LENGTH
468,214ft (142,712m)

BEAM
454,824ft (138,630m)

HEIGHT
1,218,453ft (371,385m)

PRIMARY ARMAMENT
Heavy Ion Weapon System

SECONDARY ARMAMENT
Stasis Tension Driver

TERTIARY ARMAMENT
Light Mass Fusillade Cannons

QUATERNARY ARMAMENT
Particle Cannon Network

QUINARY ARMAMENT
Anti-Ship Artillery System

Statis tension driver

Command bridge

Hull is held together by hard light bonds

Heavy ion weapon system

Composer device

Plates are capable of dynamic reconfiguration to release fighters

Mantle's Approach's attack of Earth could only be halted by the Master Chief.

COVENANT CRUISER

CRS, CCS, RCS, AND ORS CLASSES

A light cruiser isn't considered a threat in the massive shadow of UNSC *Infinity*.

The Covenant has historically held four distinct classes of cruiser, and while each looks strikingly similar in shape, their sizes and firepower can vary wildly. The Covenant's most prominent cruiser has generally been the CCS-class battlecruiser, but in the years after the war, many of those fell prey to Kig-Yar scavengers and a handful of Sangheili kaidons, hoarding whatever could be salvaged after the Great Schism. In their departure, however, CRS-class light cruisers, RCS-class armored cruisers, and ORS-class heavy cruisers came to the forefront, particularly with the reformation of the Covenant under Jul 'Mdama. During a brief but violent foray with the UNSC *Infinity* near Requiem, 'Mdama's fleet, mostly composed of light and armored cruisers, was encountered—the largest aggregation of Covenant vessels the UNSC had seen in years. Many of these cruisers were crushed in the initial assault of the shield world, but a number fled, their current location unknown.

Communications array ——

—— Point laser defense

Stasis enfolder
system

Ventral cleansing
beam/gravity lift

Hangar bay ——

Fighter
hangar bay

Both light and armored cruisers quickly leave Requiem as the shield world is being forced into its sun.

STATISTICS

CLASS PICTURED
RCS (Armored Cruiser)

CLASS LENGTH
6,562ft (2,000m)

CLASS BEAM
3,281ft (1,000m)

CLASS HEIGHT
970ft (296m)

PRIMARY ARMAMENT
Ventral Cleansing Beam

SECONDARY ARMAMENT
Anterior Plasma Cannons

TERTIARY ARMAMENT
Point Laser Defense

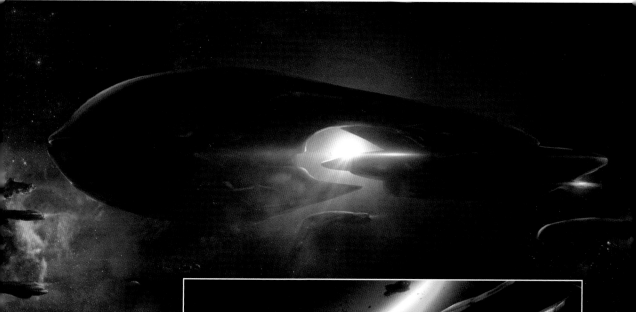

For years, the Covenant's *Song of Retribution* hung high above the surface of Requiem, searching for some way to gain access to the Forerunner shield world.

Retribution would leave *Forward Unto Dawn*'s wreckage before the Chief and Cortana managed to escape, but 'Mdama would later encounter the UNSC on the shield world itself.

SONG OF RETRIBUTION

CAS-CLASS ASSAULT CARRIER

STATISTICS

LENGTH
17,541ft (5,347m)

BEAM
6,948ft (2,118m)

HEIGHT
2,448ft (746m)

PRIMARY ARMAMENT
Ventral Cleansing Beam

SECONDARY ARMAMENT
Anterior Plasma Cannons

TERTIARY ARMAMENT
Plasma Torpedo Silo Network

QUATERNARY ARMAMENT
Point Laser Defense

After escaping the human-occupied shield world of Trevelyan (also known as Onyx), Jul 'Mdama accrued a number of vessels in an effort to form a reasonably sized fleet, awaking a remnant of the Covenant capable of engaging humanity. At its head was his flagship, *Song of Retribution*, a traditional CAS-class assault carrier capable of impressive speed and incredible firepower. Although 'Mdama used *Song of Retribution* during his initial siege of the Forerunner planet, its current location and fate remain a mystery. Despite it being evenly matched against the UNSC *Infinity* in size, 'Mdama may have been reticent to use it against the human vessel due to it being ironically outmatched in arsenal.

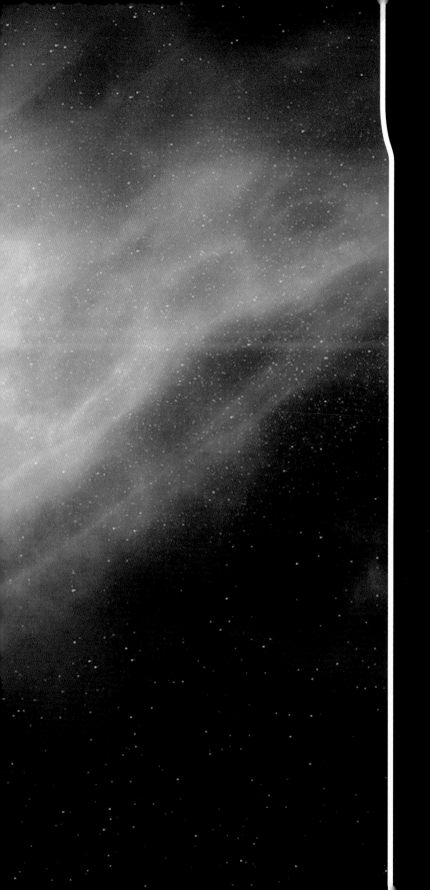

LOCATIONS

REQUIEM

FORERUNNER SHIELD WORLD 0001

What is essentially an enormous series of concentric planetary shells enclosed within each other and hidden beneath a vast armored surface, the shield world of Requiem was the Didact's main refuge during his command of the Forerunner military. Requiem would be placed in dormancy when the Didact's wife, the Librarian, discovered his crimes against the humans and betrayed him, locking him away in a Cryptum. After he was awakened, Requiem once again became a key strategic point for the Forerunner, and the UNSC would contend with this world, its extensive Promethean army, and its mysterious secrets for some time, until the artificial planet was hurled into its system's sun, Epoloch.

STATISTICS

STAR SYSTEM	**GRAVITY**
Epoloch	.987 G
SATELLITE(S)	**ATMOSPHERE**
N/A	1.2 (N2, O2, Ar)
DIAMETER	**SURFACE TEMPERATURE**
6,703 miles (10,787km)	-36°F to 159°F (-38°C to 71°C)

Within its armored exterior, the shield world of Requiem plays host to a number of concentric shells, each bearing their own surface.

Requiem's maw corridor only opens and closes from within.

Didact's ship begins its
assault on Earth.

New Phoenix was one of many well-developed URNA cities.

EARTH

ERDE-TYRENE

The homeworld of the human species and the center of UNSC power, Earth's survival at this point is nothing short of incredible. In 2552, the Covenant would at last assault this world after nearly thirty years of devastation in the colonies. Though it would be scarred by battle, Earth would somehow prevail only to encounter yet another enemy in 2557—the Forerunner known as the Didact, who would be narrowly thwarted by the Master Chief. With the bristling of civil unrest, the fomenting of another Covenant, and the possibility of the Didact's survival, Earth's future still hangs precariously in the balance.

STATISTICS

STAR SYSTEM
Sol

SATELLITE(S)
Luna

DIAMETER
7,926 miles (12,756km)

GRAVITY
1.0 G

ATMOSPHERE
1.0 (N2, O2, Ar)

SURFACE TEMPERATURE
-4°F to 104°F (-20°C to 40°C)

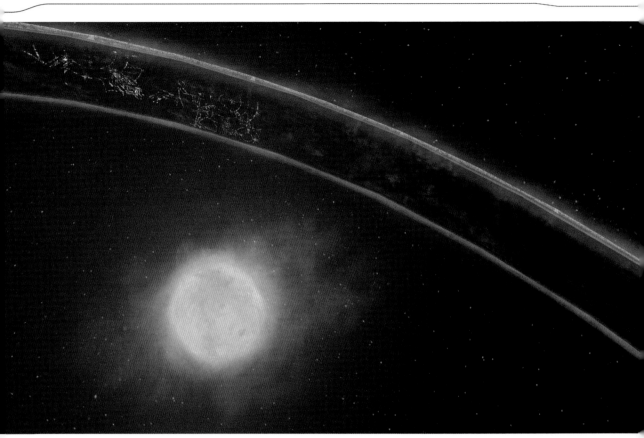

Khaphrae, Gamma Halo's sun, is a yellow dwarf star not too different from Earth's own Sol.

GAMMA HALO

INSTALLATION 03

Also known as Installation 03, Gamma Halo was discovered shortly before the end of the war. The Office of Naval Intelligence quickly established the asteroid-embedded Ivanoff Station to explore and research the ring. Early pioneer groups, accompanied by Spartan escorts, managed to quickly secure Halo's Activation Index and quarantine areas which were believed to contain the Flood. These security precautions allowed ONI to establish several excavation sites based on early seismic scans, one of which revealed a large and curious Forerunner artifact known as the Composer. This mysterious device would ultimately lead to a violent siege of Ivanoff by the Didact, and the destruction of those who lived there.

STATISTICS	
STAR SYSTEM Khaphrae	GRAVITY 1.1 G
ORIGIN Forerunner	ATMOSPHERE 1.2 (N2, O2, Ar)
DIAMETER 6,214 miles (10,000km)	SURFACE TEMPERATURE -6°F to 109°F (-21°C to 43°C)

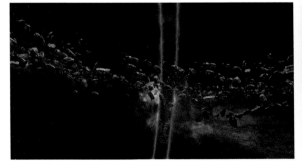

A vast and perilous chain of asteroids lies mysteriously close to Gamma Halo.

IVANOFF STATION

ONIRF IS-004920//001-54

Just before the end of the war, humanity discovered one of seven Halo ringworlds, Gamma Halo, created by the Forerunners to destroy the Flood. ONI quickly established a presence on a nearby asteroid and dubbed it Ivanoff Station, attempting to safely secure and research the Halo ring, which was also known as Installation 03. Gamma Halo held many secrets, but the most remarkable was a Forerunner artifact called the Composer, a wide-range sublimation device.

The Composer was so significant that ONI required the UNSC *Infinity* to assist in removing and transporting the artifact to Ivanoff. The device would be installed within Ivanoff's massive atrium, only to be later taken by the Didact during his assault of the station. Sadly, the vast majority of Ivanoff's personnel would be slain during this attack, either by the Covenant raiding parties or when the Didact mercilessly fired the Composer at the station.

The station's atrium plays host to the impressive Forerunner Composer recovered from Gamma Halo.

STATISTICS

ORIGIN
UNSC

SITE TYPE
Research facility

Ivanoff maintains a number of mass drivers to prevent smaller asteroids from colliding with the station.

THE CAULDRON

SITE REQ//8934-8829

STATISTICS

ORIGIN
Forerunner

SITE TYPE
Tension Modifier

Buried within a large volcanic mountain range, the Requiem site that *Infinity*'s Spartans have dubbed "The Cauldron" appears to be a thermal processing system created by the Forerunners to power large-scale tension modifiers, which are used to stabilize atmosphere pockets deep within the planet. The Cauldron was the site of numerous conflicts, and would eventually lead to the discovery of a valuable artifact the Covenant desperately sought. This object and the secrets it held made the Cauldron one of the most significant battleground sites on Requiem, later leading the UNSC to the mysterious Janus Key.

During one operation, Spartans chased Covenant leader Jul 'Mdama across the Cauldron's platform system.

Tension modifiers, such as the Cauldron's, generally rest across a shield world's equator.

Evidence suggests that the raised dais
was used by Forerunner leadership.

A spherical translocation sensor hovers eerily over the site.

THE REFUGE

SITE REQ//7848-2328

What appears to be an isolated safe
house within the Forerunner shield
world of Requiem, "The Refuge" was
a site of great interest for the UNSC
Infinity for the extent of its campaign.
Although the site's full purpose during
the time of the Forerunners remains
unknown, the Refuge's near-
inaccessibility deep within the vast

northern jungle regions of the planet
and its heavily fortified compartments
hint at it being a safe house of some
sort. The discovery of a translocation
conduit further validated this theory,
in that Requiem's occupants could
activate a portal, safely delivering them
to this site were the planet ever
besieged by outside forces.

STATISTICS	
ORIGIN	Forerunner
SITE TYPE	Safe house

Exposed power systems climb Lockup's rocky promontories.

Lockup's perimeter blends into the surrounding environment.

LOCKUP

SITE REQ//0923-4303

The key site of a number of critical ground conflicts, the location deemed "Lockup" by Spartan Command is believed to have been an enormous staging ground for midsize Forerunner vessels. Prior to deployment into war, Forerunner ships would likely coalesce at this site and others similar to it, undergoing refits, repairs, and simply preparing for flight into deep space, with actuary drones taking estimates on numbers and firepower. Data acquisitions also hint that this site may have been relevant to the first deployment of Forerunner ships during their war against ancient humans, and specifically the Didact's own ship, *Mantle's Approach*.

STATISTICS

ORIGIN
Forerunner

SITE TYPE
Naval staging ground

Not far from Apex resides Requiem's "Great Anvils"— a series of intriguing islands of impressive size.

Transit relays offer incredibly swift conveyance across the surface of Requiem.

APEX

SITE REQ//3490-9299

The vast collection of islands just off the southwestern coast of Requiem's smallest continent played host to a number of critical Spartan operations, forcing *Infinity*'s detachments to deal with both Covenant and Promethean elements throughout their protracted campaign here. Referred to as "Apex" by Command, this site appears to have once been a translocation outlier, offering individuals and machines easy access across Requiem's many environments through its incredibly large portal generator network. Scientists have since theorized that this site had other functions, as the data acquired from initial scans has offered deep insight into the Forerunners' translocation technology.

STATISTICS
ORIGIN
Forerunner
SITE TYPE
Transit Relay

COMPLEX

WAR GAMES MAP_SET/: 615-3

UNSC Galileo Base, located on the northeastern littoral coastline of Requiem's largest continent, was a critical site during *Infinity*'s protracted ground campaign in the months following the reemergence of the Covenant. Although this location was intended to be a science facility, ONI has enforced what they refer to as "Persistent Field Resilience," a mandate that requires combat readiness regardless of perceived environmental safety. This precaution would be proven well-founded, as the Covenant laid siege to Galileo a number of times, spurring multiple Spartan fireteams into action.

War Games analysts were so impressed with ONI's effectuation of the PFR mandate at Galileo that they created the "Complex" map simulation.

STATISTICS

MAP SIZE
Large

SIMULATED LOCATION
Galileo Base on the surface of Requiem

The base has been carefully embedded into the environment for safety reasons.

Galileo is perched on a remote cliff side at the base of several mountains.

HAVEN

WAR GAMES MAP_SET/: 389-4

Many worlds created by the Forerunners play host to vast ecosystems that are ultimately fed by an artificial sun. On the shield world of Requiem, such suns are formed and maintained by a massive grid of harmonic resonance platforms— intricate and powerful structures that are hidden high above the surface of the world and operate in perpetuity in order to ensure its safety. During UNSC *Infinity*'s initial scans of Requiem, the technicians captured extremely detailed scans of a number of these structures and, believing that they might be useful during combat simulations, sent them to the War Games AI for review and possible integration.

Spartan-117 was given immunity to the Composer by the Librarian at a site similar to Haven.

STATISTICS

MAP SIZE
Small

SIMULATED LOCATION
Harmonic resonance platform on Requiem

Haven's elaborate spire transmits harmonic pulses to Requiem's artificial sun.

ADRIFT

WAR GAMES MAP_SET/: 726-6

Refitted by the UNSC as an ordnance transport, this *Springhill*-class mining vessel would eventually be committed to the Battle of Kholo. During combat, the ship would be critically damaged. In an effort to find safety and gain speed, it attempted to slingshot around a nearby gas giant. Unfortunately, this act would lead to its demise, as the ship's primary engineering systems went offline, preventing it from escaping the planet's gravitational pull. Before descending into the gaseous atmosphere, the vessel sent out a number of distress signals, including a detailed systems template, which would later honor the ship's sacrifice by using a simulation of the site for training purposes.

Mining vessels, such as the CAA *Heavy Burden* saw extensive action early on during the Covenant War.

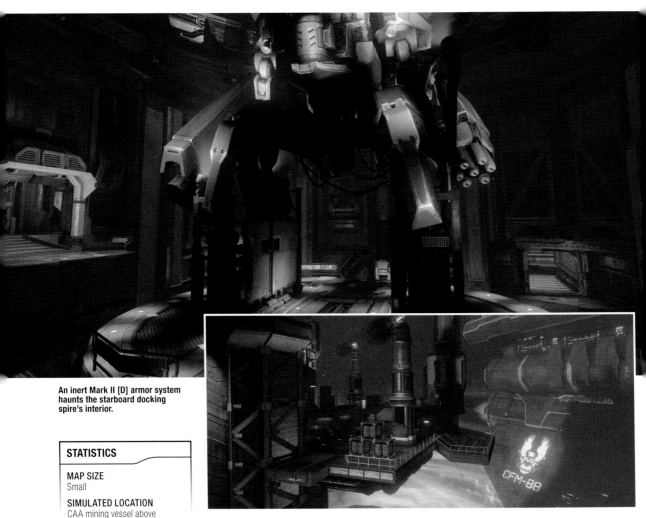

An inert Mark II [D] armor system haunts the starboard docking spire's interior.

STATISTICS

MAP SIZE
Small

SIMULATED LOCATION
CAA mining vessel above a gas giant

CAA *Heavy Burden* has two towering docking rigs on both starboard and port sides.

Longbow consists of a central hub and several outlying buildings.

LONGBOW

WAR GAMES MAP_SET/: 951-3

Given its distance from Earth, the planet of Concord is remarkably one of only a handful of worlds untouched by the Covenant War. In its northern polar regions rests Longbow Station, isolated within the frigid tundra, but it was once a hub for new discovery. In 2509, the Unified Earth Government commissioned the launch of numerous deep space monitoring relays from its twin mass drivers in order to study far-flung star systems. Eventually, this station was forced to change and began housing key military sensors that would be deployed in order to track the Covenant's movement as the enemy devoured system after system in the Outer Colonies.

STATISTICS

MAP SIZE
Large

SIMULATED LOCATION
Mass driver facility
on Concord

The driver's enormous linear accelerators reach out over the gelid Bristol Sea of northern Concord.

Solar fulcrums are the key component of stellar engineering sites such as this one.

SOLACE

WAR GAMES MAP_SET/: 992-0

Discovered by a UNSC supply ship on the border of previously held Covenant territory, this site became the source of some speculation among scientists as to its purpose and function. At the present, most believe that the powerful beacons fixed across its surface act as a solar fulcrum, capable of adjusting the energy generated by small stars. The data on this Forerunner world appears to indicate that it was once operated by stellar engineers, also known as "plasma jockeys"—Forerunners who would use facilities such as this to actually suspend the violent death of certain stars.

Atmospheric spectral dilators allows growth of native flora and fauna despite the construct's solar proximity.

STATISTICS

MAP SIZE
Small

SIMULATED LOCATION
Stellar engineering site on Forerunner world

Solace's relative symmetry lends itself to team-based combat.

ABANDON

WAR GAMES MAP_SET/: 505-2

Though Erebus VII's atmospheric conditions make it effectively habitable, it has yet to be considered a viable candidate for colonial residence due to its hostile indigenous wildlife. For some time, ONI had set up a number of research facilities across its immense equatorial forest, attempting to assess its transition challenges. When ONI lost contact with those personnel, fireteams were sent to assess the reason. They found empty facilities, with no explanation as to the whereabouts of the personnel. ONI has since suspended its efforts on Erebus VII indefinitely and has no plans to commit new resources.

The site is entirely empty, save for the bizarre, native specimens secured within.

STATISTICS
MAP SIZE Small
SIMULATED LOCATION ONI research facility on Erebus VII

Even the indigenous flora of Erebus VII exudes hostility and danger.

EXILE

WAR GAMES MAP_SET/: 784-4

Bordering UEG trade routes, this small but vibrant world had previously been undetected by humanity for centuries. When the UNSC *Diadochi*'s engine failure violently jettisoned it from slipspace, the ship's crew found themselves careening toward this planet's surface. Valiantly, these brave few managed to salvage the vessel's free fall, righting its trajectory before impact. While the crash was initially devastating, some survivors managed to pull together the ship's debris, which would provide suitable shelter for years as they waited hopefully for someone to respond to their distress beacon. Remarkably, rescue and recovery teams would later find a healthy, thriving community amid the wreckage.

STATISTICS

MAP SIZE
Midsize

SIMULATED LOCATION
UNSC *Diadochi* crash site on remote world

"Partition" eventually became the name of this world as a nod to Earth's historical Diadochi conflicts.

This centralized communications beacon relayed the crew's signal for years.

MELTDOWN

WAR GAMES MAP_SET/: 232-8

Stumbled onto by an ONI relay sensor and its science team, this frigid moon once played host to a number of Forerunner reactors believed to remotely power a distant shield world. Such technology was immediately intriguing, but as the science team would soon discover, the reactor nearest to which they had camped was undergoing a synchronization failure which would ultimately cause it to go critical, entering a thermal meltdown state. Left unabated, the icy moon, which once chilled the reactor's excessively high temperatures, would eventually be torn asunder by the site's violent and unstoppable fate.

STATISTICS

MAP SIZE
Large

SIMULATED LOCATION
Reactor canyon on Forerunner moon

Brave researchers would stay at this site for three full months, quickly gathering intel before being forced to evacuate the moon.

The site's main facilities are connected by a series of hard light bridges and tunnels.

The Requiem site on which Vortex is based is referred to as "Cyclone" by Spartan Command.

Despite its seemingly trivial function, the harvester construct is an imposing sight.

VORTEX

WAR GAMES MAP_SET/: 259-3

Perhaps the most intriguing collection of structures on Requiem, this shield world's equator plays host to a number of large-scale pressure harvesters— massive complexes that attempt to harness the planet's violent squalls for energy. The precise function of these machines remains a mystery, but some science personnel attached to pioneer recon groups believe that a proper understanding of their inner workings could yield an unprecedented amount of affordable, clean energy for the Unified Earth Government. Due to unexpected hostilities, the science teams dispatched to this site were quickly recalled after acquiring a number of detailed environmental scans for further analysis.

STATISTICS

MAP SIZE
Large

SIMULATED LOCATION
Large-scale wind harvester on Requiem

This massive tunneler structure forces atmosphere into the wind harvester.

RAGNAROK

WAR GAMES MAP_SET/: 733-4

Enigmatic and multi-purposed, spire beacons similar to these apparently frequent a number of Forerunner sites, including Halo and Shield installations, as well as the Ark megastructure. Buried within deep canyons, these towers are not only sheltered from off-world debris, but their positions allow them to leverage the steep environment's natural harmonics to amplify their signals when firing deep into space. Most scientists believe that the spires, at their base function, act as communication channels, sending specific commands to other remote locations. The full operation and over-arching purpose of these mysterious objects, however, remains a source of speculation.

This location, coined "Two Giants," would play an important role within *Infinity*'s Spartan operations on Requiem.

Ramps allow access to the spire's main platform.

IMPACT

WAR GAMES MAP_SET/: 449-2

In 2547, an ONI patrol drone recorded a violent meteor collision with an unmarked, unidentified object presumably originating from outside the galaxy. This event generated enough curiosity among top researchers for ONI to warrant dispatching a handful of EVA-ready remote contact teams. When the teams arrived, they located a large, non-native fragment of an impacting agent of unknown origin. Not only was this fragment incredibly resilient, but its material composition was highly irregular, unlike anything ONI had ever encountered before. Even more intriguing, the object's age appears to indicate that it originates well prior to that of the earliest of known Forerunner artifacts.

STATISTICS

MAP SIZE
Varies

SIMULATED LOCATION
ONI archeological site on remote asteroid

The existence of this site is linked to the discovery of a relatively small fragment of rock with very mysterious and ancient origins.

Despite the immense size of this environment, the ONI facility occupying it is relatively small.

This elaborate platform likely provided access to the large defensive construct buried below the planet's surface.

RAVINE

WAR GAMES MAP_SET/: 982-3

During a number of classified planetside expeditions conducted in this part of Requiem, specific teams were dispatched in order to ascertain the purpose and function of the many citadels towering over this tropical sea. To their surprise, a series of deep-sensor seismic scans revealed that the structures were actually part of a far larger construct hidden below the sea. Assumptions among analysts vary, but the most widely accepted theory is that the citadels are rampart-like towers rising above the apex of the hidden Forerunner creation, somehow acting like automated battlements of an impossibly large castle.

STATISTICS

MAP SIZE
Varies

SIMULATED LOCATION
Large-scale citadel rampart on Requiem

This beautiful, pristine sea belies the terrible purpose of these towering edifices.

An overwatch station rests high above the site's primary facility.

This supply bay's beacon tower relays data to hundreds of probes distributed across the planet's surface.

EROSION

WAR GAMES MAP_SET/: 773-9

In the aftermath of the Covenant War, the UNSC became proactive in pioneer efforts to locate new worlds, particularly in light of millions of human refugees who had somehow managed to escape from their fated colonies. Early on, they discovered Eudemon X49-05. The moon's composition was actually quite viable during initial tests—oxygen-rich, water-plentiful, and teeming with life of all kinds— easily comparable to Earth's makeup. However, all of this was overshadowed by the moon's tectonic activity, which was irregular and potentially problematic. To learn more, research teams were deployed into its cavernous interiors in order to assess any potential risks with colonization.

STATISTICS

MAP SIZE
Varies

SIMULATED LOCATION
Lunar pioneer site on Eudemon X49-05

HARVEST

WAR GAMES MAP_SET/: 309-8

Peaceful, serene, and sparsely populated, the farming colony of Harvest had no real defense to mount against the merciless Covenant invasion that began in 2525. Prior to the five-year war that would follow, the colony's most spectacular site was arguably the tether complex—a series of seven strands mounted just outside of the city of Utgard and terminating at Tiara Station, many kilometers above the planet's surface. At the base of each space elevator were numerous agricultural machines and systems, each conducting countless automated functions that would benefit not only this world, but dozens of others.

The tethers connecting to Tiara were controlled by the AI Sif, who managed all of Harvest's immense shipping operations.

Space elevators have a variety of designs based on function, layout, and purpose.

STATISTICS

MAP SIZE
Large

SIMULATED LOCATION
Tether base of Tiara Station on Harvest

In the distance, large machines manage individual crop sectors, guided by Mack, Harvest's agricultural operations AI.

SHATTER

WAR GAMES MAP_SET/: 593-6

The architects of the original Mjolnir powered assault armor are the government-contracted technology firm known as the Materials Group, based out of Damascus, on the remote world of Chi Ceti IV. Of this world's two moons, Muroto was the only one deemed viable by the Materials Group for the specific type of mining they required, which, in actuality, led to their choice of Damascus. It was discovered early on that Muroto was incredibly rich with a particular light-weight, heavy-grade crystal needed for augmenting various armor composites. However, the company's sites there have now been victims of a number of setbacks due to a series of unrelenting storms and perilous volcanic activity.

The Materials Group has had a significant mining presence on Muroto for several decades.

After the addition of a number of weapons and vehicles, scans of this site have allowed War Games combat simulations to be conducted here.

STATISTICS

MAP SIZE
Midsize

SIMULATED LOCATION
Materials Group facility on the moon Muroto

Despite the volatile meteorological conditions of Muroto, Chi Ceti at dawn is still an incredible sight to behold.

Some translations have referred to this as the Forerunners' "Maginot Line," harkening back to certain defenses of post-World War I France.

WRECKAGE

WAR GAMES MAP_SET/: 893-3

Referred to by the Forerunners as Jat-Krula, the Line was an immense sphere of defensive installations, which comprised the barrier of a critical fallback point during their prodigious war with the Flood. These Line installations, parsed in fours, composed a massive sphere-like territory, which would use a number of technologies to trap, seize, and destroy any unsanctioned vessels. Line Installation 9-12 was recently discovered by scavengers when their ship was trapped on its surface. Setting up makeshift camps in its debris field, they had hoped to secure treasure, but all that remains now of their bleak transmissions are detailed environment scans of their final resting place.

The debris on these installations spans the gamut of ship types, including human, Covenant, and even a number of undiscovered species.

STATISTICS

MAP SIZE
Midsize

SIMULATED LOCATION
Line Installation on remote Forerunner world

The Spartan teams deployed during the Battle of Casbah were not contemporary S-IVs, but from the legendary S-II and S-III classes.

LANDFALL

WAR GAMES MAP_SET/: 891-3

The planet of Tribute was one of the most prominent commercial colonies in all of human-occupied space. Its fall in 2552 marks one of the great defining tragedies of the war, but it has also served another purpose. During one of the last battles in the capital city of Casbah, a single Spartan fireteam would hold off a brutal torrent of Covenant ships in order to provide refuge for a handful of escaping civilians. The urban, portside warrens of this battleground have since been catalogued as part of the War Games simulation and are regularly used for training in homage to the great sacrifice made by a brave few.

STATISTICS

MAP SIZE
Midsize

SIMULATED LOCATION
Port facility in the city of Casbah on Tribute

The port facility's command center remains eerily empty in light of the Covenant's attack.

Casbah saw impressive economic and commercial growth during the late 25th century, leading to ports such as this one.

Sothra Hakkor's enormous visage bears down upon Monolith's surface.

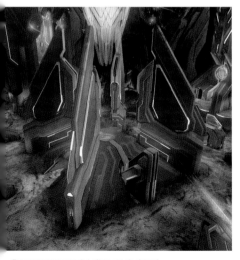

Forerunner memorial sites are designed to evoke awe and reverence.

MONOLITH

WAR GAMES MAP_SET/: 673-4

Acquired from incredibly precise environment scans stored on Requiem, this particular location is believed to be a monument for Forerunner warriors shortly after their long forgotten war with ancient humans. In the aftermath of this great conflict, the Didact personally ordered that a number of these towering structures be built throughout the system, including the narrow asteroid field slung near the core world of Sothra Hakkor, where this site apparently resides. While the validity of this hypothesis may be questioned, the scans acquired are incredibly compelling and clearly convey the majesty of Forerunner architecture.

STATISTICS

MAP SIZE
Small

SIMULATED LOCATION
Ancient Forerunner memorial site on asteroid

SKYLINE

WAR GAMES MAP_SET/: 490-2

Set atop the impressive skyline of Cascade's capital city of Mindoro, several major corporations have joined together in the construction of a massive space tether. Terminating at Station Nova Austin, which currently orbits high above the city, this elevator system will become a critical link for off-world transit and shipping, making it the world's most important commercial spaceport. Despite the adjacent rooftops' relative safety, security drones have determined that its particular layout is optimal for infantry combat training and have subsequently incorporated it into a number of UNSC and ONI simulation programs.

Defense contractor Lethbridge Industrial was one of the leading manufacturers responsible for the tether's construction.

<table>
<tr><td colspan="2">STATISTICS</td></tr>
<tr><td>MAP SIZE
Small</td></tr>
<tr><td>SIMULATED LOCATION
Tether build site in Mindoro on Cascade</td></tr>
</table>

Mindoro's immense cityscape is a sight almost unparalleled on any other UEG colony world.

This facility is an outlier of the larger research platform looming in the distance, which in turn is only a small part of Oban's full ONI presence.

Even non-combat facilities are required to meet certain military-grade specs.

DAYBREAK

WAR GAMES MAP_SET/: 902-5

STATISTICS

MAP SIZE
Midsize

SIMULATED LOCATION
ONI research facility on remote world of Oban

This particular research site is safely nestled atop an eyrie in Saviron's northern highlands.

The majestic, blue-green world of Oban is without question impressive and will eventually serve as a home to millions of human refugees currently stuck in between worlds. In the northernmost highlands of the vast continent of Saviron, a cluster of ONI research facilities and sensor relays participate in Operation: DAYBREAK. This relatively modest planetside effort will help prepare the world's surface for rapid colonization efforts in the coming years. In the interim, the UNSC Navy continues to use its gravity well as a staging ground for highly classified military campaigns in neighboring systems.

Unsanctioned military complexes such as this one are primarily functional in constitution, usually eschewing all cosmetic presentation.

OUTCAST

WAR GAMES MAP_SET/: 822-2

The Outer Colony of Talitsa has always had a strong anti-centralization and pro-colonial autonomy sentiment, but over the past years, UNSC intervention—however unfortunate—became necessary, particularly during a series of uprisings in its major population centers. The results of this military action were less than ideal, with many outlying rebel sects coalescing into larger and stronger groups before escaping into Talitsa's hardscrabble outlands to create a number of heavily armed redoubts.

Some of these sites have been discovered by the UNSC, but many remain well-hidden, sparking concern within the upper echelons of the Unified Earth Government.

STATISTICS

MAP SIZE
Large

SIMULATED LOCATION
Rebel base in the distant outlands of Talitsa

Rebels have procured a number of useful vehicles including this armored cargo transport.

The Pilvros' rail transport system runs extensively throughout the entire city.

Reactor warrens are always off-limits to the general public.

PERDITION

WAR GAMES MAP_SET/: 755-3

Far below New Carthage's city of Pilvros, one of the metropolis' key reactors has suffered a systemic failure. This critical condition will eventually become a meltdown, violently devouring everything above it in a massive expenditure of energy. With confirmation that this crisis could not be avoided, local security has invoked a mandatory, city-wide evacuation. In the recesses of the reactor complex, however, a team was deployed to acquire detailed scans of the entire area. The hope is that new data might offer some answers to the reactor's mysterious failure in an effort to prevent other tragic and costly incidents in the future.

Current environmental scans show the reactor in the throes of meltdown, violently expelling energy and debris.

STATISTICS

MAP SIZE
Midsize

SIMULATED LOCATION
City reactor site in Pilvros on New Carthage

GLOSSARY

The Halo Universe is teeming with acronyms and terminology that could not be effectively articulated throughout the course of this book. In order to aid the reader, here is a light glossary that will provide some insight into words or names that you'll want to be acquainted with.

Acheron Security
A human ordnance and materiel manufacturer based out of the city of Gdynia, on the colony of Mars.

Achoem Weapons
A Sangheili-founded ordnance and materiel manufacturer based out of Tolvuus, on Sanghelios.

Actium A human colony founded in 2397, but lost to the Covenant in 2545.

Activation Index A device used to activate and fire a Halo ring.

Ancilla An artificial intelligence created by the Forerunners

APFSDS Armor-Piercing Fin-Stabilized Discarding Sabot

APGJDU Armor-Piercing Gas-Jacketed Depleted-Uranium

ASGM
Automatic Self-Guided Missile

ASW Anti-Ship Weapon

A/X Atmospheric/ Exoatmospheric

BDU Battle Dress Uniform

Boglin Fields A human corporation which manufactures ship engines.

CAA Colonial Administration Authority: The previous administrative body for humanity's colonies, established in 2310.

CAMS Corbulo Academy of Military Science: An esteemed military academy for select UNSC youth, located on Circinius-IV.

CDS Chalybs Defense Solutions: A human ordnance and materiel manufacturer previously based on the now-glassed colony of Meridian.

CMA Colonial Military Administration: The previous military and policing body for humanity's colonies, established in 2310.

CNM Command Network Module

ComL Incendiary material used for human-made anti-infantry explosives.

Composer A Forerunner device capable of transforming a living being into raw data.

Covenant A collection of alien species religiously dedicated to the discovery of Forerunner artifacts. Believed to be defeated by the UNSC in 2552, a newly formed fanatical version of this alliance reappeared only a few short years later.

DAYBREAK An ONI military operation conducted on the planet Oban in order to prepare it for colonization.

Delta-Six A classified military division of highly trained forward deployed operators.

DEM Directed Energy Mortar

DESW Directed Energy Support Weapon

DEW/L Directed Energy Weapon/Linked

DEW/M Directed Energy Weapon/Mounted

DEWE Directed Energy Weapon Emplacement

DHMG/FM Dual Heavy Machine Gun/Flank-Mounted

Domain An ancient Forerunner database operating as a transcendent quantum repository for information and history.

DTPF Deuterium-Tritium Pure Fusion

EMP Electromagnetic Pulse

EVA Extra-Vehicular Activity, as in actions taking place in the context of space or other zero-gravity scenarios.

Fireteam Majestic A key Spartan fireteam aboard the UNSC *Infinity*.

Flood An ancient, extra-galactic parasite that engaged the Forerunners many millennia ago, eventually forcing them to fire the Halo Array.

FMJ-AP Full Metal Jacket - Armor Piercing

FOF Friend-or-Foe tag, usually appearing on one's heads-up display to indicate friendly and hostile entities nearby.

Forerunner An ancient race of highly advanced beings who were believed to have perished during the activation of their Halo weapons many millennia ago.

FSC Flood Super Cell, as in a base material that comprises pure Flood.

FTP-HE Ferric-Tungsten Projectile - High-Explosive

G/GNC Grindell/Galileian Nonlinear Cannon

GAU Gun, Aircraft Unit

GEN1 First Generation, referring to Mjolnir armor previously worn by Spartan-IIs and Spartan-IIIs.

GEN2 Second Generation, referring to Mjolnir armor generally worn by all contemporary Spartans.

HAAW/M Heavy Anti-Armor Weapon/Mounted

Halo Array A series of enormous ringworlds created by the Forerunners, which were in essence powerful weapons used to destroy the Flood. When fired, this array is capable of rendering the galaxy completely empty of all sentient life.

HEI/AP High-Explosive Incendiary/Armor-Piercing

HEI/RD High-Explosive Incendiary/Remote Detonated

HMG/AM Heavy Machine Gun/ Anti-Materiel

HRG Heavy Rail Gun

HUD Heads-Up Display: An arrangement of intel provided to UNSC personnel via their helmet's visor.

HV/FTHPP High-Velocity/Ferric -Tungsten Hollow-Point Projectile

HVE High-Velocity, Explosive

HWS Hannibal Weapon Systems: A human ordnance and materiel manufacturer based out of the city of Kotka, on the colony of New Carthage.

Imbrium Machine Complex
A human ordnance and materiel manufacturer based out of the city of Ankara, on the colony of Luna.

Insurrection A series of civil conflicts between the UNSC and human colonies which began in 2494.

Jat-Krula The collection of Line installations created by the Forerunners, based on a previously abandoned military philosophy established earlier in their history.

Jaunt-Combat Excursions A type of deployment that involves numerous brief military operations conducted over a short period of time and generally in one theater of war.

Jiralhanae A pseudo-ursine species originating from the world of Doisac, joining the Covenant in 2492 CE. Also known as "Brutes."

Kig-Yar A pre-avian species with saurian roots originating from the world of Eayn, joining the Covenant in 1342 CE. Also known as "Jackals" or "Skirmishers."

Kradal Conflicts A series of battles conducted by the Forerunners long before the Flood War.

LAAG Light Anti-Aircraft Gun

LAM Laser Aiming Module

Lekgolo A vast collection of eel-like organisms originating from the satellites around Te, joining the Covenant in 784 BCE. Also known as "Hunters."

Lethbridge Industrial A human ordnance and materiel manufacturer based out of the city of Lethbridge, on the colony of Concord.

Lifeworker A rate within the Forerunner species focusing on the care and preservation of all living things.

Line installation An artificial world created by the Forerunners to generate a defensive barrier against the Flood, though it ultimately failed. These installations worked by forcefully downing or outright destroying any vessels that passed nearby.

MAC Magnetic Accelerator Cannon

Materials Group A human ordnance and materiel manufacturer based out of Damascus, on Chi Ceti IV.

MBHRC Multi-Barrel Heavy Rotary Cannon

Misriah Armory The leading manufacturer for human ordnance and materiel within the UNSC, its primary sites are located on Mars.

Mjolnir A highly advanced armor used by Spartans, referred to as MJOLNIR when referencing the classified military project.

MLA Machine-Linked Autocannon

MLRS Multiple Launch Rocket System

MMG Medium Machine Gun

MOUT Military Operations on Urban Terrain

MP Munitions Projectile or Military Police

Naoto Technologies A human corporation which manufactures ship engines.

Naphtali Contractor Corporation A human ordnance and materiel manufacturer based out of the city of Abilene, on Earth.

Navy Special Warfare Group A group within the UNSC Special Forces, including early SPARTAN programs, ODST, and other military projects.

Neural donor An individual who donates their neural physiology as a framework for an artificial intelligence construct.

New Phoenix A city within North America which was the site of the Didact's vicious assault in 2557, leaving the entire area empty of human life.

ODST Orbital Drop Shock Troopers, a select group within UNSC Special Forces which focuses on deployment behind enemy lines, usually via orbital insertion.

ONI Office of Naval Intelligence: an elite administration which manages numerous classified military operations within the UNSC, established in 2178.

Ordnance Commission A post-Covenant War military commission headed by major armor defense companies in May 2553 and sponsored by ONI.

PEW/M Projected Energy Weapon/Mounted

RED FLAG A high-risk naval operation planned in August 2552 in order to end the war, but was ultimately aborted due to the Covenant's attack on Reach.

San'Shyuum One of the founding species of the Covenant and the collective's former leadership prior to the Great Schism. Also known as "Prophets."

Sangheili One of the founding species of the Covenant, previously the military command though now maintaining all leadership roles. Also known as "Elites."

SAP-HE Semi-Armor-Piercing - High-Explosive

SBHVC Smooth-Bore High-Velocity Cannon

SBHVC/DM Smooth-Bore High-Velocity Cannon/Dorsal-Mounted

SGML/AM Self-Guided Machine-Linked/Anti-Materiel

SinoViet SinoViet Heavy Machinery, a human technology and transportation company.

Shield installations A defensive world or structure created by the Forerunners to protect against both the Flood and the firing of the Halo Array.

Skirmisher A more avian genetic alignment within the species Kig-Yar, similar to their cousins, the Jackals.

Spartan A genetically enhanced and cybernetically armored super-soldier of one of four projects. The most common and recent is Spartan-IV, though some Spartan-IIs and Spartan-IIIs remain active.

Special Operations Classified military operations conducted by highly trained soldiers, also considered the military division that contains these specific soldiers.

SSM Surface-to-Surface Missile

ST Self-Tracking

Terceira A human colony which saw a major revolt led by the United Rebel Front. It was recovered shortly after by UNSC forces.

TS Tactical Shotgun

UEG Unified Earth Government: A centralized governing administration for all human territories, including solar and extrasolar colonies, established in 2075.

Unggoy The lowest species found within the Covenant originating from the world of Balaho, joining the Covenant in 2142 CE. Also known as "Grunts."

UNSC United Nations Space Command: The UEG's primary military force established in 2164.

UNSC High Command The highest governing office of the military organization known as the UNSC.

URNA United Republic of North America

Ushuaia Armory A human ordnance and materiel manufacturer previously based on the colony of Reach, destroyed by the Covenant in 2552.

VISR Visual Intelligence System, Reconnaissance: Currently the most up-to-date HUD software used by UNSC personnel.

War Games Competitive military simulations generally performed by Spartans on a highly advanced combat deck, using pneumatic risers and holographic images to recreate real-world environments from previously collected environment scans.

X-HP-SAP Experimental - High-Powered - Semi-Armor Piercing

XO Executive Officer

INDEX

Main entries highlighted in bold.

LONDON, NEW YORK, MUNICH,
MELBOURNE, AND DELHI

Senior Editor Victoria Taylor
Editor Zoë Hedges
Design Manager Maxine Pedliham
Senior Designer Clive Savage
Designers Owen Bennett, Alison Gardner,
Simon Murrell, Lisa Robb
Managing Editor Laura Gilbert
Publishing Manager Julie Ferris
Art Director Ron Stobbart
Publishing Director Simon Beecroft
Pre-production Producer Rebecca Fallowfield
Producer Danielle Smith

First published in the United States in 2013 by
DK Publishing
345 Hudson Street,
New York 10014

13 14 15 16 10 9 8 7 6 5 4 3 2 1
001-193685-Oct/13

Published in Great Britain by Dorling Kindersley Limited.

A catalog record for this book is available from the Library of Congress.

ISBN: 978-1-4654-1159-4

Color reproduction by Alta Image
Printed and bound in China by South China

343 Industries would like to thank Christine Finch, Mike Gonzales,
Kevin Grace, Tyler Jeffers, Kiki McMillan, Carlos Naranjo, Tiffany O'Brien,
Frank O'Connor, Jeremy Patenaude, Corrinne Robinson,
and Annie Wright for bringing this book to life.

Additional 343 Industries thanks to Scott Dell'Osso, Josh Holmes,
Matt McCloskey, Bonnie Ross-Ziegler, Phil Spencer, Kiki Wolfkill, and
Carla Woo, as well as Axis Animation, Bungie Studios, Certain Affinity,
Digic Pictures, and The Sequence Group.

343 Industries would also like to thank Stephen Loftus,
who provided his expertise and insight into the Halo Universe
for the betterment of this book.